BROOKLYN WAS MINE

RIVERHEAD BOOKS

New York

BROOKLYN
WAS MINE

Edited by
CHRIS KNUTSEN
& VALERIE STEIKER

RIVERHEAD BOOKS
Published by the Penguin Group
Penguin Group (USA) Inc.
375 Hudson Street, New York, New York 10014, USA
Penguin Group (Canada), 90 Eglinton Avenue East, Suite 700, Toronto, Ontario
M4P 2Y3, Canada (a division of Pearson Penguin Canada Inc.) • Penguin Books
Ltd., 80 Strand, London WC2R 0RL, England • Penguin Group Ireland,
25 St. Stephen's Green, Dublin 2, Ireland (a division of Penguin Books Ltd.) •
Penguin Group (Australia), 250 Camberwell Road, Camberwell, Victoria 3124,
Australia (a division of Pearson Australia Group Pty. Ltd.) • Penguin Books India
Pvt. Ltd., 11 Community Centre, Panchsheel Park, New Delhi—110 017, India •
Penguin Group (NZ), 67 Apollo Drive, Rosedale, North Shore 0632, New Zealand
(a division of Pearson New Zealand Ltd.) • Penguin Books (South Africa) (Pty.)
Ltd., 24 Sturdee Avenue, Rosebank, Johannesburg 2196, South Africa

Penguin Books Ltd., Registered Offices: 80 Strand, London WC2R 0RL, England

Permission to excerpt letters and notes in "Reading Lucy" by Jennifer Egan
courtesy of the Brooklyn Historical Society; Alfred Kolkin and Lucille Gewirtz
Kolkin Collection, 1942–1965, the Brooklyn Historical Society.

First Riverhead trade paperback edition: January 2008

Library of Congress Cataloging-in-Publication Data

Brooklyn was mine / edited by Chris Knutsen and Valerie Steiker. — 1st Riverhead
trade pbk. ed.
    p. cm
  ISBN 978-1-59448-282-3
  1. Brooklyn (New York, N.Y.)—Description and travel.   2. Brooklyn (New York,
N.Y.)—Social life and customs.   3. City and town life—New York (State)—New
York.   4. Street life—New York (State)—New York.   5. Authors, American—
Homes and haunts—New York (State)—New York.   6. Authors, American—
New York (State)—New York—Biography.   7. New York (N.Y.)—Description
and travel.   8. New York (N.Y.)—Social life and customs.   I. Knutsen, Chris.
II. Steiker, Valerie.
  F129.B7B823 2008
  974.7'23043—dc22   2007037006

PRINTED IN THE UNITED STATES OF AMERICA

10 9 8 7 6 5 4 3 2 1

What is it then between us?
What is the count of the scores or hundreds of years between us?
Whatever it is, it avails not—distance avails not, and place avails not,
I too lived, Brooklyn of ample hills was mine . . .

—WALT WHITMAN, *Crossing Brooklyn Ferry*

CONTENTS

INTRODUCTION
Phillip Lopate

NOT SO MUCH when world-weary as when I'm feeling chipper, I saunter over from my house to the Union Street Bridge, to take in the restorative waters of the much-maligned Gowanus Canal. I live on Sackett Street, one block north of Union, so first I walk over to Union Street and then go left, past the modest brick three-story homes with their stoops and stone angel fountains and religious decorations and patriotic American flags and an occasional Italian tricolor, this being a longstanding Italian neighborhood, where gangster Al Capone grew up and immigrant stevedores labored on Brooklyn docks to raise a roof over their families' heads, with a renter downstairs. These are not the fancy brownstones nowadays selling for several million, but awkward, cozy row houses, whose lack of cachet increases as you approach the canal. Essentially, no one of class ever wanted to live near the Gowanus, legendary for its stink and for mobsters' bodies fished out of the canal; rumor had it that if you were unfortunate enough to fall in, your bones would be dissolved by acids instanter.

The old Gowanus creek had been enlarged in the 1840s to service nearby factories and move construction materials for the burgeoning habitations of Brooklyn; and this dinky little canal, one hundred feet wide and less than a mile long, no deeper than fifteen feet in high water, became one of the most trafficked watercourses of nineteenth-century America. By then it had already become so polluted an 1893 newspaper could call it an "open cesspool." In the twentieth century, it devolved into a one-use channel—a conveyer of heating oil, whose toxic leakage into the creek bottom and the nearby shores' sediment complicated any future development for recreational or residential uses. They would all have to be treated as "brownfields" and laboriously cleansed at enormous cost. This daunting proposition has not prevented local community planners from fantasies of converting the lowly Gowanus Canal into Little Venice, with outdoor cafés hugging the narrow banks. (Inshallah, it will never happen.) The tides being too sluggish to rid the channel of pollutants, a flushing tunnel has been installed, whose pumping action goes a long way toward alleviating olfactory insult. Domestic oil continues to be transported intermittently by barge, necessitating the raising of the Union Street drawbridge, a pokey operation that leads local drivers to lean on car horns and curse their fate. There is also another Gowanus Canal drawbridge, two blocks south on Carroll Street, older and more charmingly wood-planked, with verdant views almost Last-of-the-Mohicans primeval; but for some reason I keep being lured to the funkier Union Street Bridge.

Standing on the span, looking outward toward the north, I see what is most astonishing for this city: a good deal of sky and clouds above low-scaled structures, and a vast sweeping view of Brooklyn that would have quickened the pulse of any Delft landscape painter. You can luxuriate in the profligate empty space ("waste," to a developer's eye) framed by the canal. At the canal's northern terminus fly the national and city flags of the NYC Department of Environmental Protection substation. In the distance, the deco crown of the Williamsburgh Savings Bank Tower, the tallest building in Brooklyn, at one time its only legitimate high-rise, and until recently a haven for dentists' offices, though now being inevitably converted into condos, towers over the Wyckoff Houses, a public-housing complex whose white-brick facades make it appear more hopeful or at least less stigmatized than the usual grim red project brick of the Gowanus Houses, glowering to the right. On the canal's western bank, a small grassy meadow with wild-flowers, bisected by oil pipes, slopes down to the greenish, petroleum-iridescent water. Along the eastern bank are lined the back ends of mostly abandoned factories, painted with graffiti and faded words like "Conklin Brass." The *thump-thump* of cars passing over the bridge's metal plates contributes to the contemplative mood.

If I cross the road and look south, toward Red Hook,

there appears a parking lot filled with Verizon telephone trucks, in the distance the elevated trestle of the F train, and the "Kentile Floors" sign, and a factory placard that reads "Alex Figliola Contracting: Water Mains and Sewers." Across the bridge, on the Park Slope side, is a proliferation of auto-body shops. All this prosaic attention to infrastructure and repair, strewn haphazardly on either side of the canal amid weeds and ailanthus trees, this strange combination of industrial, residential, and bucolic, speaks to the plain, somnolent essence of Brooklyn. The genius of Brooklyn has always been its homey atmosphere; it does not set out to awe or intimidate, like skyscraper Manhattan—which is perhaps why one hears so much local alarm at the luxury apartment towers that have started to sprout up, every two blocks, in those parts of the borough lying closest to Manhattan. Much of the chagrin is expressed by people who have moved here from elsewhere; I, a native Brooklynite, never romanticized the place as immune from modernity, nor do I see why such an important piece of the metropolis should be protected from high-rise construction when the rest of the planet is not. But my feelings are mixed: for if the sleeping giant Brooklyn were to awake and truly bestir itself and turn into a go-getter, I would deeply regret the loss of sky. Perhaps it is some deep-seated, native-son confidence that Brooklyn will never quite get it together, which allows me to anticipate its bruited transformation with relative sanguinity. Meanwhile, I stand on the Union Street Bridge, a fine place from which to contemplate the Brooklyn that was, that is, and that is to be.

NOT just a place, Brooklyn has become an idea, a symbol, and a contested one at that. The nineteen contributors in this collection, all highly esteemed writers, grapple with its meanings in the pages that follow. Let us throw out a few key notions that recur in these essays, as a starting point: history, immigration, home and exile, neighborhood, public space, pastoral, loss.

The pull of history, local and personal, is very strong, especially for second- and third-generation Americans. Jennifer Egan connects with this past by researching a woman named Lucy who worked in the Brooklyn Navy Yard; Elizabeth Gaffney rhapsodizes a time when "Brooklyn's sewers were the gold standard" of the nineteenth century; Darin Strauss investigates his great-grandfather's boast that he played baseball for the Brooklyn Kings; Joanna Hershon compares her romantic memories of the Brooklyn Bridge with those of her grandmother. Katie Roiphe lovingly links up her father's Depression-era Coney Island with her own. Many of the authors represented here had parents who grew up in Brooklyn, only to flee it for more upwardly mobile climes. "From my father's perspective, still after all those years, he'd gotten us *out*—a reverse exodus of heroic proportions, mixed with dashes of startling good luck—and the idea that a son of his would choose to live in the Old Country, where he'd been poor and miserable, was something he couldn't quite fathom or accept," writes John Burnham Schwartz. Alexandra Styron, who also had to counter her famous writer-father's mystified reaction to her ending up on the "wrong" side of the East River, writes, "What could young Bill Styron have known of Fuhgeddaboutit Brooklyn Pride? Or the silent fellowship enjoyed by those of us, a generation later, who have *escaped* Manhattan?"

These writers have come back to redeem the promise of ordinary life, as inculcated in them by their sires' ambivalent tales. Often they display a filial or grand-filial reverence for the haunts and enjoyments of their ancestors' youth that borders on the curatorial. Recalling the old days when egg creams reigned supreme, Emily Barton hunts down the last seltzer delivery man left in Brooklyn: "[W]e like having the crates and bottles in our kitchen, a tie to this city's past. I like the connection to my father's childhood, my aunts' and uncle's childhoods, and a world that was based around neighborhoods, where you knew the people who lived next door and ran the shop around the corner."

In our day—with the metropolis threatened by forces of globalization, cyberspace, and suburbanization—the word *neighborhood*, as the locus of mundane, face-to-face encounters, has taken on a quality of almost mystical longing for a vanished ideal, side by side with its continuing existence as reality in a few places, such as . . . Brooklyn.

Hence the palpable ache behind these accounts of the fragile, quotidian miracle of neighborhood life, as in Susan Choi's description: "Underwood Park, from the very beginning, has reminded me of a piazza, a little town square. It's the only public space in the city that has given me friends that I cherish, and the means to retain them, as well. Now that we're parents we're so busy, we can never do things, we can never see people . . . except for our comrades of Underwood Park. Here we constantly meet, in the interstices between what we imagine makes up our 'real' lives, but this life, we have to admit—this endless throwing and retrieving of a ball, this endless cycle of shade trees to acorns to the winter hiatus from which our kids burst, metamorphosed completely, while we try to believe we ourselves haven't aged—is the real life: the repetitive rhythm, the onrush of time."

For newer immigrants, displaced from half a world away to these bizarre shores, like the Ethiopian-American writer Dinaw Mengestu, the promise of community embedded in a Brooklyn neighborhood is even more poignant: "It didn't take long for me to develop a fierce loyalty to Kensington. . . . I knew the hours of the call of the muezzin that rang from the mosque a block away from my apartment. I heard it in my bedroom every morning, afternoon, and evening, and if I was writing when it called out, I learned that it was better to simply stop and admire it. My landlord's father, an old gray-haired Chinese immigrant who speaks no English, gradually smiled at me as I came and went, just as I learned to say hello, as politely as possible, in Mandarin every time I saw him. The men behind the counters of the Bangladeshi takeout places now knew me by sight. A few, on occasion, slipped an extra dollop of vegetables or rice into my to-go container, perhaps because they worried that I wasn't eating enough."

According to Mengestu, the "very absence of grandeur" allows him to feel at ease in the streets; he has earned his place, he belongs here: "The haphazard gathering of immigrants in Kensington had turned it into a place that even someone like me, haunted and conscious of race and identity at every turn, could slip and blend into." In multicultural Brooklyn, where no one will look at you funny if you speak with an accent, it is indeed possible to blend in. Not that everyone feels equally accepted. Neighborhoods acquire identity as much by exclusion as by inclusion: witness the occasional Brooklyn riot when someone of the wrong color strays into a block where he is not wanted. And the preservation of immigrant cultures can take on a self-conscious, caricatured air, as Lara Vapayar wittily observes: "Everything Russian on Brighton Beach is too Russian, far more Russian than in real Russia. This is what happens all over Brooklyn. From the Scandinavians of Bay Ridge to the Chinese of Sunset Park, Brooklyn's immigrants go to ridiculous extremes to re-create their homelands only to end up with a vulgar pastiche."

Still, here is actualized the improbable ideal of a place where the whole world can live together in more or less harmony. Brooklyn works. That is the message that comes across time and again in these personal essays. Darcey Steinke entitles her lovely piece about moving into a neighborhood near Prospect Park "Brooklyn Pastoral." Lawrence Osborne, fresh from Bangkok, rides his bike around the peaceful streets of Red Hook; Rachel Cline revisits the pool at the St. George Hotel; and Robert Sullivan watches the wind play its tricks in downtown Brooklyn. These authors are, as Stendhal once put it, nostalgic for the present. They value so much of what they have that one keeps waiting for the other shoe to drop—for something bad to happen. The title of this collection, *Brooklyn Was Mine*, set in past tense, implies that, yes, something is about to be lost, some possession or identity taken away. The poet Vijay Seshadri puts it beautifully: "Almost without my noticing it—or rather, almost without my being able to register the shifting music through the dense curtain of urban sound and sense—the neighborhood has changed, leaving me with the commonplace but nonetheless sharp recognition that I only began cherishing it when I understood it was disappearing."

Jonathan Lethem's wild, sardonic screed, "Ruckus Flatbush," imagines Brooklyn with a dystopian future. Philip Dray summarizes the coming apocalypse in a more measured tone: "Today, the area is rapidly losing its working-class, bohemian flavor and becoming a cookie-cutter bedroom community for Manhattan, its sepia past closing like the iris dissolve at the end of a silent film." Yes, well, maybe so. We ought to remember, though, that the wealthy—far from being a new barbarian army invading— always maintained a presence in Brooklyn, with sumptuous villas and mansions. The borough was never simply the quaint working-class/bohemian heaven it is sometimes presented as being: there were always social hierarchies and class tensions, as well as large pockets of the most uncharming poverty.

Who is to say what will become of the place, or whether Brooklyn will retain its soul? I like to think it will. In any event, we can take heart from the eloquent writing in these pages, which proves that whatever happens to Brooklyn as a built environment in the near future, its literary soul is sound and robust, and its writers fiercely loyal.

I HATE BRIGHTON BEACH
(A Conflicted Love Letter)

Lara Vapnyar

I HATE BRIGHTON Beach. This is the first thought that comes to mind whenever someone mentions the place. I imagine myself behind the wheel, stuck in the honking traffic on Brighton Beach Avenue, hopelessly searching for a parking space, trying to squeeze past all the double-parked cars, trying not to run over people with overstuffed shopping bags who cross without paying the slightest attention to the light, after a while not caring if I run them over or not, sometimes even wishing that I do. I imagine the gloomy brownstones and the ugly metal stakes, the rumble of the subway overhead and the smell of gasoline, rotting vegetables, smoked fish, and garlic marinade. I imagine the sharp wind coming from the ocean, and gray boardwalk, and cold sand "the color of carpet in a New Jersey home," as I described it in one of my stories. But most of all I imagine the inexplicable sense of embarrassment that washes over me every time I see myself as part of the Brighton Beach scene. And yet, whenever I set my foot on a Brighton Beach Avenue sidewalk (after I have finally managed to find a parking space), I experience a strange, almost painful kick of pleasure, a deep forceful thrill.

Years ago, when I first came to the United States from Moscow, I used to work on Brighton Beach. I lived in the Midwood area of Brooklyn. It took me about ten minutes to drive to Brighton Beach from there, and about twenty minutes to find a parking space. I hated my job. I hated it because accepting that job meant giving up on my American Dream, which centered on finding an interesting, meaningful job, something that would match my high esteem of my own talents and expertise, something like teaching Slavics on a college level, or becoming a film critic, or writing insightful essays for serious American publications. My husband and all my Russian friends and relatives who came to the United States at the same time as me had all already found "real jobs," prestigious, well-paying jobs, more or less matching their college degrees in science and technology. They worked in Manhattan, in big buildings, in nice clean offices, with Americans. My degree was in humanities, and I quickly found out that it didn't count for anything at all. I was twenty-three, and we already had a baby, so we couldn't afford for me to spend time and money on getting another degree in humanities, an American one, and possibly just as useless. I had a choice of taking a quick class and learning a useful profession (something like medical billing or accounting) or finding a temporary job with one of the Russian businesses. The first option was rational and reliable, but I chose the second one, because I hoped that it would buy me some time to figure a way to do something closer to my dreams. I knew that if I found a stable job as an accountant or some such, there would be no escape.

I worked in a tiny two-story house, squeezed between other such houses on a cramped dirty street off Brighton Beach Avenue. A white sign in front said "Alternative and Holistic Medicine" in big Russian letters, and "Witchery and Magic" in smaller ones. I shared my office space with people who sold some magical tea that was supposed to cure every ailment but was in fact simply a laxative, with a healer who was aptly named Ludmila the Grave, and with a woman who was advertised as "authentic witch from the woods of western Ukraine." I wasn't much better than they were. My English was far from fluent, but I faked my diploma and got a job as an English teacher for elderly Russian immigrants. "It's okay, they won't know the difference," my boss told me after he heard me speak in English. My goal was to teach them the bare minimum of English, just enough for passing the citizenship exam. Most of my students were in their seventies and eighties, none of them knew any English. They had terrible memories, hearing problems, and blood pressure that would shoot to dangerous highs at the mere thought of learning English. So I taught them how to pretend that they knew English. Fortunately, there were only so many possible questions that the INS officers could ask them. I taught them the answers suitable for most of those questions. "If the officer asks you something, and you don't understand anything, not a word, say this: 'My name is . . . , I was born in . . . , I came to the U.S. in . . . , I like the U.S. because it's a free country." I also encouraged them to slip the few English expressions that they knew into the conversation. "Say that the weather is beautiful, or if the officer is a woman, say, 'You're beautiful.' They would think that you know at least some English." It took them weeks to memorize "you're beautiful."

And then my class would be over and I would walk back to my car parked on Brighton Beach Avenue, thinking that everything about Brighton Beach was as fake as my teaching methods.

BRIGHTON Beach is called Little Russia, or Little Odessa, but there is hardly anything there that would evoke Odessa, Moscow, or any of the small Russian towns that I've been to. Brighton Beach does not look, smell, or sound like Russia. It's a parody of Russia at best, something as different from the real thing as a picture of the Eiffel Tower on a souvenir mug is from the real Eiffel Tower. Yes, they sell Russian food on Brighton Beach, and Russian books and videos, and Russian clothes, and there are Russian restaurants and Russian nightclubs, and everybody speaks Russian, but the Russianness of the place is so concentrated that it feels ridiculously exaggerated. Everything Russian on Brighton Beach is too Russian, far more Russian than in real Russia. This is what happens all over

Brooklyn. From the Scandinavians of Bay Ridge to the Chinese of Sunset Park, Brooklyn's immigrants go to ridiculous extremes to re-create their homelands only to end up with a vulgar pastiche.

Every time I walked down Brighton Beach Avenue, I felt that there was this huge stamp on me saying "RUSSIAN," just as loud and obvious as everything else on Brighton Beach. I felt that this stamp would never allow me to really fit in American life, and I felt embarrassed of having to carry it and ashamed of being embarrassed.

So, yes, it isn't difficult to pinpoint all the things that make me hate Brighton Beach, and to come up with a logical explanation of why I do. It is far more difficult to explain why I have always felt that strange pleasant kick, that buzz of excitement on Brighton Beach, and why I still feel that way every time I am there. Perhaps the cause of my problem is that everything that is wonderful about Brighton Beach is wonderful precisely because it defies logic.

Look at the store signs, for example. Don't pass them by. Read them carefully.

CAVIAR KIOSK—DON'T FORGET TO MAKE YOUR KEYS. I have stared at this sign for a long time trying to figure out the connection. Keys and caviar. Keys and caviar. Caviar and keys. What could it be? You can make a magic key that gives access to all the caviar you can eat? Caviar as a key to your physical and emotional well-being? Turned out that there wasn't any connection whatsoever. I entered a regular ninety-nine-cent store with its usual assortment of plastic dishes, plastic toys, and batteries. But they did have a locksmith's window in the back and a caviar stand in front, in the right corner. At the caviar corner there was a glass cabinet, like the one you see in a pharmacy, or in a doctor's office, only filled with caviar instead of medicine. With all kinds of caviar imaginable. Beluga. Sevruga. Osetra. In blue tin cans, and red tin cans, and jars, and even in large plastic containers, some kinds plausibly expensive, others suspiciously cheap. Stock up on your caviar and don't forget to make spare keys.

Or this sign across the street from the caviar kiosk.

THEATER TICKETS. SILVER AND STEEL JEWELRY. NAILS. NAILS. NAILS.

Uh-huh, a person buys a ticket to a show, and then remembers that he has no good jewelry to wear to the theater? But why steel? For what kind of performance would anyone want steel jewelry? And what about those nails? Do they mean fingernails? Or steel nails, pegs, bolts? Must be steel nails if they are already selling steel jewelry. But no, this turned out to be a tiny manicure salon with a theater ticket booth attached and a small window where they sold jewelry made from silver and steel.

Still, my favorite sign was the one they used to have above a little café. The sign read PEL'MENI (dumplings) in Russian and CAPPUCCINO in English. Now the word *cappuccino* is missing from the sign, probably because it moved to a recently opened Starbucks down the street.

There is something wickedly wrong about having a Starbucks on Brighton Beach; for some reason it strikes me as more wrong than Starbucks in, say, Paris. Few establishments are more sound, correct, and somber than Starbucks. Few establishments clash with the spirit of Brighton Beach more.

All the other food places have a certain element of wackiness that Starbucks lacks, which makes them just right for Brighton Beach, be it a huge restaurant that looks more like a funeral home or a tiny hole-in-the-wall where they sell tea with lemon in paper cups and all kinds of *pirozhki*. After class, I would buy myself two (my favorite was the one with the cabbage and onion stuffing) and eat them on the way to my car. The *pirozhki* felt heavy and warm, and it was somehow comforting. I would try to wipe my hands well, but the grease would still get on the steering wheel.

But the best, the most affecting, the most absurd, and the most heartbreaking thing about Brighton Beach has always been its true denizens—Russian elderly. They are not as noticeable on weekends and after hours, when Brighton Beach Avenue is teeming with successful Russians who come from the city and well-to-do suburbs to stock up on Russian food and culture. But on weekdays Brighton Beach is rightfully theirs.

There they are. Some are my former students. Couples bickering in Chinese vegetable stores. Men—playing either chess or dominoes on the boardwalk. Other men watching, shouting their advice, arguing. All dressed in baseball caps and ill-fitting down jackets. Women—some sitting in groups of five or six on folding chairs by the entrances of the brownstone apartment buildings. Wearing knitted hats of all the possible brilliant colors. Watching the outside world and judging it sharply. Other women strolling along the boardwalk in pairs, wearing fur coats and bright makeup and haughty expressions. Some moving with the help of walkers. I don't know, there is something painful and uplifting at the same time about the sight of women with walkers wearing fur coats and coral-red or magenta lipstick. Something that makes your heart skip a beat.

The amazing thing was that many of my students did pass their citizenship exams. Nikolay Semenovhich, eighty-three, came to tell me the good news with a bouquet. He gave me the flowers, then scrunched up his face and began kneading his forehead in a desperate attempt to recall something. In a few minutes it came to him.

He said, "You are *feautibul.*"

This was screwed up and ridiculous, but so touching and defiant at the same time. It was pure Brighton Beach.

I left my Brighton Beach job when my second child was born. By that time I had all but given up on my dreams and was set on learning computer programming. And at some point while I sat staring at the computer screen and trying to make sense of the code, a really wacky idea came to me. Why didn't I try to write fiction in English? This was completely crazy, because I had never written fiction before, in any language, and I spoke English with a monstrous accent and tons of grammatical mistakes, but I had nothing to lose and I tried. When my first story appeared in the *New Yorker*—and that was a true miracle—one of my American friends said, "What should I do to get published in the *New Yorker*? Screw up my English?" Well, yes, sometimes this is the only thing you can do to achieve the impossible—screw up your language, and defy your logic and learn how to use "nails," "theater tickets," and "caviar" in one sentence. I learned that on Brighton Beach.

My kids are now twelve and nine. Sometimes, I bring them to Brighton Beach, and they like it there. They like the beach, and the books in the stores (they pick the ones that have the minimum amount of text, like *Origami Manual* or *Dinosaur Atlas*, because it's hard for them to read in Russian). They love Russian pickles, Russian bread, and Russian salami. They are not embarrassed or stirred by Brighton Beach. And the reason for that is very simple—they are not Russians. They are Americans. But I do hope that one day they will be able to see what Brighton Beach is all about.

READING LUCY

Jennifer Egan

LAST SPRING I formed a brief, powerful friendship with a woman named Lucille Kolkin. She was a Brooklynite, like me. For two months, Lucy and I spent a couple of hours together at the Brooklyn Historical Society every Wednesday and Friday, while my son was at preschool in the neighborhood. I say two months, but in Lucy's life it was actually five—from April to September 1944, when she moved to California and we lost touch.

We met for professional reasons. I was researching a novel I'm writing about a woman who worked at the Brooklyn Navy Yard during World War II, and Lucy actually *worked* at the navy yard for almost two years, as a mechanic in the shipfitting shop. When she started, in the fall of 1942, she was Lucille Gewirtz, but within a year she'd met Alfred Kolkin, from the mechanical shop, and married him after a brief courtship she once jokingly referred to as "Maidenhood to Marriage in Three Easy Months." The speed doesn't surprise me; Lucy was passionate. It's one of the things I love about her.

By the time I got to know her personally, I'd already spent time with the lecture notes she took at navy yard shipfitting school. She wrote in blue pen in a small loose-leaf binder, defining countless acronyms (WL=waterline; AE=after end; FE=forward end) and neatly diagramming ships in cross-section. Since I, too, was trying to learn the basics of battleships, I began copying down much of what Lucy had copied, including details like: "Construction is started at midship and continued on both sides of it. Balances weight." But I also encountered flashes of the life attached to the notes I was cribbing from:

> *Buy–Bag*
>> *Shoes*
>> *Bras*
>> *~~Stock~~. ~~Dye~~*

> *Fix–~~suit~~*
>> *gray dress*
>> *blue suit*
>> *stocks*

> *From cleaners—coat*

Who was this woman whose to-do lists looked so much like mine? I knew that the historical society had a collection of correspondence between Lucy and her husband, beginning in April 1944, when he joined the navy. I requested the first group of letters she'd written to Alfred when he left for boot camp in Sampson, New York. That was when our friendship began.

Lucy wrote to Alfred almost daily—often on the streetcar she took from Twentieth Avenue in Bensonhurst, where she ate supper at her mother's house before beginning her night shift at the navy yard. "We're approaching Pacific St. again—(wish I had a longer ride)" was a typical sign-off, accompanied by endearments: "Oodles of love and about 7 little kisses," or "So I'll throw in another kiss and just an inchy winchy pinch on the aft end." She was wildly in love with her husband. "You're a huge success, fella," she wrote to him on May 4, 1944. "Not only I—but the other thousand girls in the yard think you're handsome. See, I've been sporting a new picture of you and in my characteristically 'proud of my husband' feeling, no one can escape seeing it."

On an undated letter in May, she kissed the paper she was writing on in a spectacular shade of pink lipstick. It was shocking to see the impression of her lips, every crease still visible after sixty-two years, as if she'd left it ten minutes before.

Lucy described herself as a shipfitter 3/c, meaning third class, ("buzz: soon, to be 2/c I think," she told Alfred in June), and she often seemed to have the aid of a "helper," also female. A shipfitter fabricates and lays out the metal structural parts of a ship—a job that it would have been laughable to think of a woman performing before the war. But as male employees at the yard were drafted or enlisted, someone had to replace them; the Brooklyn Navy Yard was the largest shipbuilding facility in the world during World War II. It built seventeen battleships and repaired five thousand, including Allied ships from all over the world. And by January 1945, there were 4,657 women at the yard, working in nearly every phase of shipbuilding and repair.

I was hungry for detailed descriptions of Lucy's shipfitting work, but as is often the case when someone talks to a fellow "insider," her remarks about work were mostly in passing: "stenciled 120 pieces for a job" or "I was put back on the flow this afternoon—and I didn't like it nohow." She liked being the timekeeper, which apparently happened every two weeks and allowed her to stay in the office and write letters to Alfred. She complained often of sore feet (later mitigated by a pair of rubber-soled shoes) and described her hands as "kind of scratched." In one of her longest descriptions of actual work, from July 17, she wrote: "First it's 4, then it's 1, then it's 6. No, I ain't talking about babies—or even the time. You see, I'm a shipfitter and I'm making up some more kingposts and booms. 'Make up 4.' So I start making up the fittings for four ships. 'Cancel 3, they're duplications.' So I put some fittings for three ships away in case I get the job again. Then I make up the rest of the fittings—enough for 1 ship. 'New order. Make up six.' So I start pc#1, pc#2 all over again. It's not a bad job otherwise." She included a diagram of a kingpost, with an arrow indicating a "5 × 5 H Beam about 9' lg."

When it came to life in the navy yard *around* the job

itself, Lucy was superb. "I just learned of a wonderful way to lose friends—and get a lot of laughs—or do you already know the funnel trick?" she wrote in an undated letter. "Near closing time this morning, the boys said that for 10c a try a fellow could put a half dollar on his fore-head, a funnel in his pants and if he got the 50c piece into the funnel by bending his head it was his. Well of course when he put his head back to balance the coin, a container of water was poured into the funnel. Some level of humor!"

She had a particular interest in union organizing (she referred occasionally to "union friends") and also in the plight of "negroes," whom she viewed with great sympathy. Here's an anecdote from her letter of May 3:

"Yesterday, Minnie, a negro tacker who has been in the yard as long as I and interested in becoming a fitter, became disgusted and signed up for welding school. Another victory for Haack [Lucy's supervisor] and his ilk. Poor gal—she hates welding and is all upset. She knows she's not doing the right thing by giving up the fight but she insists there's nothing else to do. A couple of negro girls and I were trying to talk her out of it. But she persists in the idea that not only does she have to fight as a woman, but as a negro. She was practically in tears . . . She's a former teacher and math genius—and Gee! Butch, it's such a God damn shame."

Four days later, she wrote: "Just learned Minnie (remember?) is not quitting shipfitting. Our little talk with her took effect."

Amid the news, anecdotes, and political and cultural observations that Lucy somehow managed to pack into these daily missives, I learned the basics of her life: she and Alfred were Jewish. Lucy had gone to college—at Hunter—while Alfred had not, which occasioned from his wife occasional pep talks about how little college really mattered: "I went to college. So what. I look for a job and people say, 'Yes, yes but what can you <u>do</u>?' 'Nuttin' say I.'" She also had a habit of footnoting words whose meanings Alfred might not know—like *querulous*—and providing definitions. In one letter she included a lengthy tutorial on how to read music. The instruction apparently went both ways; in another letter, she asked Alfred for directions on how to wire a room.

I found these letters deeply absorbing; not only did hours pass without my noticing, so that I often found myself huffing, flustered, to pick up my son, but often it felt like sixty-two *years* had passed without my noticing—such was the ringing immediacy of Lucy's voice. In some ways our worlds felt close together: we walked the same streets (I live in Fort Greene, a few blocks from the navy yard); we both worked hard and struggled to find time for practical necessities like cleaning and shopping. Like me, Lucy hated buying clothes; "I'll brand myself, I'll go before a firing squad—anything," she wrote to Alfred in April. "Only I won't try on another dress." She loved movies and live performances, which in her case meant Duke Ellington, Paul Draper, Danny Kaye's *Up in Arms*, and countless

other movies. And she often reported on her avid reading:
Dorothy Parker, Howard Fast, Boris Voyetekhov's *The Last
Days of Sevastopol*.

Of course, Lucy was much younger than I am—in her
midtwenties, in the early phase of her adult life. Part of the
pleasure of reading her letters was wondering how her life
would turn out; would Alfred return to Brooklyn, or would
they put a down payment on a house in San Francisco, as
Lucy fantasized? Would she continue to work, or leave that
behind for motherhood? Would she have children? Would
her love for Alfred remain as heedless as it was in this first
year? I mused with an odd sense that these answers
couldn't be known—as if Lucy's life, like mine, were still a
thing in motion, with many outcomes uncertain. That's
how close she seemed.

Sometimes, while crossing the street or jogging over the
Brooklyn Bridge, I would have the thought that I might
actually *see* Lucy, not as she was now—however that might
be—but the Lucy of 1944: wisecracking, a talker, drinking
a strawberry malted. I was dying to hear her speaking voice
(I imagined it deep and a little crackly) and to see what she
looked like beyond that fuchsia print of her lips. All of
Brooklyn seemed full of her.

On May 7, Lucy wrote, "Butchie—guess what! I had
a dream last night about our having a baby—a couple of
months old—cute + blond—and dressed in a regular
basque shirt + shorts. You were diapering him and I suggested it was about time you taught me how to diaper him,

etc, etc. I should know better than to disclose my dreams, but it was too nice to keep to myself. Anyway, I guess the dream belonged to you too."

After reading that sentence, I stood up suddenly, walked to one of the historical society computers and typed "Lucille Kolkin" into Google. Within a second or two, I was reading her obituary. She'd died suddenly, in 1997, at age seventy-eight. She'd had two daughters, two grandchildren, and lived in New York. After fifty-three years of marriage, Alfred had survived her.

I returned to my seat, shaken. It was one of those moments when technology crushingly outpaces cognitive reach; I couldn't seem to make the transition from the handwritten pages in front of me, full of blindness and hope, to the obituary on the screen. It was several minutes before I resumed reading Lucy's letters, and when I did, it was at a slightly treacherous remove, as if I were withholding information from her—like faking surprise at an outcome you already know.

After that, I found Lucy's letters poignant in a way that they hadn't seemed before. As she prattled to Alfred about bicycling in Prospect Park or rubbing bicarbonate of soda on the sunburn she'd gotten on a trip to Coney Island with her girlfriends, it would cross my mind that I knew the time and place of the death that awaited her. And I felt a corollary awareness as I walked the Brooklyn streets, holding my little sons' hands; how old would they be when I died? Would they have had children of their own? How would they remember me? Lying in bed with my husband, the big tree swaying outside, I thought about Lucy's words to Alfred: "the glorious blossoms on the tree facing our window—that is <u>the</u> tree in Brooklyn. The last thing I say good-morning to before sleeping." It made me eerily conscious of a point of view from which our lives would look quaint, and a long time ago.

Meanwhile, in 1944, events in Lucy's life were rapidly unfolding: Alfred began radio technician training in Chicago, and Lucy gave up the little apartment they had shared and moved in with her mother. There was much speculation about where Alfred might be stationed next, and the news came in August 1944: he was moving to a naval base in Del Monte, California. "The news of your new destination is not too bad," Lucy wrote to him. "I understand the climate there is very much like heaven . . . Perhaps I can go to the Yard in that state—altho it's about 150 miles from where you'll be. They work on 8 hour shifts there—and I imagine I'll be able to see you every week-end."

Two days later, she deemed the California Navy Yard "no good—too far away," but shortly after that, she revived the idea of a transfer. "I'm pretty certain I could get a transfer to the Calif. Navy Yard," she wrote on August 6. "If you can't sleep out and the Yard is within a 150 mile radius—I almost think it pays to get a transfer. The Yard is near San Fran.—a nice place to live—and 150 miles is really not too far to travel. What do you think?"

The reaction from Alfred must have been cool, because

six days later, Lucy wrote, "Butch, do you really object if I feel like you? After all, you wanted to enlist even tho it meant leaving me. Well, I feel I have an important job too. And I don't feel like dropping everything and working in Del Monte just now—especially since I'll hardly be able to see you anyway. But if I work in San Fran. I can continue the work I'm doing and be able to see you besides."

I already knew the outcome of this debate from the biographical note accompanying the letters: Lucy would follow Alfred to Del Monte and work as a waitress. There would be no letters for almost a year, although they would begin again when Alfred shipped out in 1945. Still, as I read, I found myself mentally exhorting her the other way, as if the decision still hung in the balance, as if I could yank her, physically, from her time into mine. *Go to the yard,* I imagined telling her. *Savor this fluke of independence before the clamp of 1950s domesticity closes around you. Bank some more skills to capitalize on when the sexual revolution hits in twenty years. Please, Lucy, get the transfer! Go to San Francisco. I grew up there; it's gorgeous.*

The resolution came three days later:

". . . went to see my doctor—first time in about 5 weeks," she wrote, apparently referring to a therapist. "I was discussing my confused ideas about going to Calif. And thru association we discovered why I was confused—but my sub-conscious seems bent on going. Ain't this silly talk? But I like it. And so I'm still going. I plan to leave about the middle of September. Are you happy?"

The remainder of this section of Lucy's correspondence was mostly consumed with the details of her departure: packing with her girlfriends, the decision of whether to go by Pullman (expensive) or coach; the good-bye presents she was given by the women she worked with at the navy yard (books); the composition of her luggage. She mentioned a referral from the navy yard that she could present to the San Francisco Navy Yard, should she choose to. On September 5, on her way to Chicago—the first leg of her cross-country train trip—she wrote: "I showed some of your pictures to one of the girls on the train. She's seventeen and thought, 'you're a dream.' Yeah? Not for long, Butch. Soon you'll be a reality and then we'll both be happy."

Then, the letters stop. In the first days without her raucous writing voice and her panoramic gaze, I felt a little lost. I found myself contemplating tracking down some of her living relatives—her two daughters and maybe Alfred, if he was still alive—so I could talk to them about the rest of her life: the time between age twenty-six, where I'd left her, and seventy-eight. But that seemed a strange expenditure of time and energy, given that I was supposed to be researching the Brooklyn Navy Yard. In the end I settled on reading some of Alfred's letters to Lucy, beginning at the same time that hers had begun, in April of 1944. And as soon as I began reading, I felt relief: Alfred was a hoot. He had all of Lucy's humor and intelligence; his riotous account of learning to swim in navy boot camp made me laugh out loud. I'd conjured Alfred as a faceless 1950s drone, but I should have trusted Lucy—she would never have picked a guy like that. Soon after beginning Alfred's letters, I felt myself begin letting go, preparing to leave these two extraordinary people to live out their lives together.

The last letter I read of Alfred's involved plans for his furlough to Brooklyn in early May:

"I'm looking forward to those five days together Lucy," he wrote. "I want us to cram a lot of things into it. It'll be easy if we plan it a little bit . . .

"I'll take you swimming in Hotel St. George Pool and you can see what progress I've made. I'll show you how a sailor rows a boat. I'll show you what a 'boot' can do to a good home-cooked meal. And you'll see that I can dance as flatfootedly as ever.

"You'll see!"

RIDING IN RED HOOK

Lawrence Osborne

TO LEAVE A city for another is to invite a harrowing return. After a year in Bangkok, I returned to Brooklyn, not knowing what to expect and, even worse, not knowing how to move like a local. It is tantamount to saying that I didn't know what to remember, and it was akin to ending one relationship and beginning another.

I began by buying a bike, an antique Peugeot. I thought perhaps that a bike would lessen the shock of moving from one city to another, would help me forget the streets I missed so much in Asia. Already, walking around Brooklyn at night I felt sorely abandoned to myself, sinking like a stone into some clutching boredom. The only sign of wildlife I could find near me was outside the Salvation Army outlet on Bond, where men high on meth shout along to music and tap-dance opposite the Goodwill donation store. It's joy of a sort, the nearest thing to the wildness of a Bangkok street.

Brooklyn felt spacious, pious, half-empty. I couldn't get the hang of it. I couldn't get over the way the sidewalks

offered ample room for three people abreast, or the way
you could rush down them without hurtling into tables
piled with cilantro, sugar pots, and dancing hookers. I was
astonished by the wind, the nonstop sirens, the verticality
of those proud, brittle churches. It was like a devout village
that has solved even the problem of dog shit—and most
surprising of all there was no vice, no decadence, and no
sex. Certainly, there were men screaming "Fuck you,
bitch" on the street outside my bedroom, but that is not
quite sex, is it?

Where did one eat *guaytio* soup on the street at three in
the morning? Where did one go for a three-hour hot stone
massage at midnight? The carnal appetites? You go home
quietly, you lock yourself inside your apartment, and you
pick up a magazine if you suffer from a little insomnia.
There's nowhere to go, and so you behave. You behave
because you are not ingenious, and because you are afraid
of the police.

One of my friends in Bangkok was a Jewish aid worker
from Brooklyn called John Purdoe, who works at the main
AIDS charity hospital in the Klong Tuey slums. We were
driving through a Bangkok traffic jam one night and he
confessed to me that he had never missed Brooklyn after
a decade in Asia. Why not? A motorbike with two girls
flashed past our window, and as they passed us they smiled
at him for no reason, as people on two wheels do in
Bangkok, with sexual intent with no ulterior motive.
"That's why," Purdoe said. "*The come-hither look.* Try get-

ting a come-hither look in Brooklyn, except from a drug dealer."

No matter. I came back to Brooklyn to try to salvage a failing relationship, and come-hither looks on Bangkok's streets were immaterial. Perhaps I could salvage something if I survived a summer of biking without losing a leg like the dismal hero of Coetzee's *Slow Man*.

The bike turned out to be a stroke of genius, and if the truth be told it was the suggestion of the estranged girl-friend. She must have suggested it as a therapeutic measure to cope with the abrupt end of an already short relationship that my absence in Bangkok had rendered impossible. I felt guilty about it, and the bike became a sort of atonement. I cycled hard, pouring out all my misery on two pedals and a pair of brakes.

I raced pointlessly around Red Hook and the water-fronts, around Fort Greene and the repetitive wastelands of Bay Ridge. It was like flogging myself with nailed whips, because the fact is that I dislike bicycles, and I especially dislike the sight of myself on a bicycle, where I look like a wartime British air-raid warden waiting for a finaliz-ing bomb. There is something a little sanctimonious about bicycles, something gratingly superior. They are the trusted vehicles of vicars.

But now there developed a strange chemistry between the absence, the lover, and the bike. And then, out of the blue, the disappearing lover called to ask if we *could go on a bike ride together*. I didn't refuse, though I couldn't see what the point of it now would be—the relationship itself was broken beyond repair, and the request made no sense except insofar as it was an invitation to explore something together with the meandering delicacy of a bike ride, which never has a precise objective. It came after months of quarrels and absences and finally silence. What would a bike ride cure?

We exchanged possible routes by e-mail, and this shared virtual map reading itself became a reassurance that neither of us was dead or forgotten to each other, at least not yet. It was not clear why we should do this, or why the back streets and forgotten neighborhoods of Brooklyn should be the places where our love affair could peter out of its own accord, like something pulled by gravity down a long slope toward a resting place from which it will never recover. Look, she seemed to be saying, we could have been doing this while you were wasting us away in Bangkok, a city where I could never have trusted you for a moment, not in the world capital of the come-hither look! But that was not quite it.

We planned to ride to Coney Island, but never did. Other, even more ambitious routes, never came to fruition. I wondered what I would say to her in this moving situation (in both senses of that adjective). Can one talk freely and intimately on the bike path, trespassing through traffic lights, avoiding SUVs and children, and overtaking prams? Or was this an invitation to rediscover the city itself, at least a small corner of it—as if I lacked it in some way and by lacking it had missed something on the way to breakup?

There are places in New York that take you back to Bangkok. Vinegar Hill, for example, with its gaunt power stations and warped streets, the sense of industrial decay that has continued too long to rewind. It is the sadness of the nineteenth century, which outside of Europe was a century of imitation and unease. For New York, like Bangkok, was no London or Paris—it was a place of desperate striving and Darwinian commerce that left behind these zones of warehouses and ruins, of canals thick with heavy metals and typhoid. They have a decomposed quality that induces a sweet pessimism in the bicyclist.

The streets of Red Hook are even more Bangkokian as they exhaust themselves at the water like the broken alleys of a riverside neighborhood such as Wang Lang: Van Dyke with its lofty skeletal structures and its Valentino Pier, the battered wharves and destroyed jetties around the Flickinger glassworks and the old Northside bottling center. Thoroughfares like Creamer and Halleck and Otsego with their bird's nests of cables: it is the same man-made forest look. The canal and its tributaries in Gowanus recall the *klongs,* which run underground all over Bangkok, and which make it a water city.

I found that she was a little unfamiliar now, like someone you have seen too many times in a single photograph who suddenly appears at your door. In bright sunlight she

looked more ravaged, and therefore more explicable—
but that was an impression that could reverse itself in a
moment.

We set off like a Victorian picnic party, genteel and awkward. It was a ride in which little was said, because there is
usually very little to say. Riding was a way of getting around
this looming silence by filling it up with sight-seeing. We
rode down to the very ends of streets like Bond and Court,
which are known for their more lively parts inland, and it
was satisfying to see how they ended—Bond Street tapers
down to a cobbled cul-de-sac by the canal just where the
erector-set sign for Kentile Floors rears itself above Robert
Moses's freeway. From this side, the words appear backward, like some vague threat from *1984*. On a sign hung
from the canal fence is the following instruction: "If you
see discharge during dry weather call 311." It was not a
number I would ever be using.

Here the skies are always brilliant, crossed by soaring
trains and by the tracery of dead trees. Strange little com-
panies have their quarters here, things like Fireproof Door
Company and Cyberstruct. As we went round and round,
we passed the formidable mass of Treasure Island storage
on Center Street, which asks you to "Store Your Treasures
Here" and offers you a large painted palm tree as an incen-
tive. Hardly exchanging a word, we sailed down Bay and
Bryant until we were in the shadow of one of the buildings
I love most in New York, the abandoned grain terminal. It
looks like a Crusader castle in the Middle East, Krak des

Chevaliers perhaps, with the mysterious graffiti word *BARONE* painted across it. Beautiful in its sinister hugeness, it silences the passerby. And on the far side of it one comes to the humble finale of Court Street, little more than an alley running past loading bays for the Hass oil company and ending at the prickly barriers of the U.S. Coast Guard.

This is the quietest place in the city, so close to the sea but separated from it by a mass of chimneys, warehouses, and bright-red pipes and taps with fire-hazard warnings. Turn a corner and you hear the water lapping at ruins. I rode behind her, and all this time I followed the outline of the body, so familiar in the way it slanted to left and right, the violin form with—so to speak—its tightened strings, and now untouchable, like something moving off in the dark. We stopped at Halleck next to the Keyspan yards, where we saw a row of chocolate warehouses swept by dried up vines, and I gave her a tense, squinted glance. It began to occur to me that this wandering was a form of farewell, one in which hands would not be raised or words exchanged.

There were moments to get off and sun, for example at the lovely corner of Sigourney and Otsego, where no one comes and where metal chimneys stand in shining rows. Further on is Coffrey Street, whose buildings have the liver-red oxide color of African roads. A drink at the Liberty Heights taproom, delightfully estranged as a pub can be, and then a slow meandering down Van Dyke, where one can see the Clay Retort and Fire Brick house, built in 1854 by the superbly named Joseph K. Brick. It looks like a small Tuscan church made of gray schist, which was how it was designed, and it reminds you that people once bothered to build brick factories in the image of Tuscan churches.

As the ride progressed, I began to feel happier, more curious about the place where I lived but which I didn't really know. The love affair lost its subtle preeminence for a while, and I let my eye drift up tall brick chimneys slender as Egyptian steles, along lines of cemented windows and boxes of Fafard Canadian growing mix piled along a waterfront. There are moments when a city can suddenly acquire all the kinetic qualities of a human being, a person's moods and expressions, so that she becomes a character of some kind—like a large woman, I often think, half asleep on her side. You find yourself talking to her, asking her questions, pestering her. And living in such a city is a long, monogamous affair, or else a marriage one abandons from time to time. Cities are rarely casual flings.

We went into the new Fairway down by the water, which must now be the largest supermarket in Brooklyn. It is a surprising labyrinth of gourmet pretension in such a neighborhood, and we wandered down aisles as long as subway platforms, half lost, perusing and window shopping and bitching about the cherries and not really shopping at all, just passing time and gossiping about the price of grapefruits and favorite coffees and the infuriating stick-

iness of plastic grocery bags. It was all curiously anticli-
mactic.

And then we stopped by the cheese counters and there
was a moment when I caught her staring down for a
moment at a Stilton, and there was something tired and
sad in the mouth, an immense age, and I realized that in
some way she had simply been borne away by the flow of
ordinary life. If I had met her in a restaurant or in the usual
bars I would never have seen it, and I would never have
seen it if I had never bought an old Peugeot.

Our bike ride was not the last time I saw her, but it was
almost the last, and it was the farewell that never otherwise happened. And I thought of Auden's line the next
time I rode alone along Van Dyke, which does not remind
me of her at all: "Hearts that we broke long ago have long
been breaking others."

A SENTIMENTAL EDUCATION
Alexandra Styron

*In those days cheap apartments were almost impossible to find
in Manhattan, so I had to move to Brooklyn.*

—WILLIAM STYRON, the first line of *Sophie's Choice*

THE FIRST TIME I read these words I was thirteen years
old, and my father's novel, which he'd spent most of my
conscious childhood years writing, was just out in galley
form. Intrigued and proud (the advance word on the book
was, I knew from talk around the house, excellent), I took a
copy to school in my book bag. During breaks in the day—
recess, study hall—I began to read *Sophie's Choice* in a
conspicuously serious fashion, hoping to attract interest in
Me and My Father's Extremely Important Achievement
from a maximum contingent of the school population. As it
turns out, no one was much interested in what I was doing,
least of all me. I found the book mind-numbingly boring.
The difficult vocabulary and historical references went
mostly over my head; it became a bitter struggle just to
keep my eyes from glazing over entirely.

Until I got to page 47.

It was on or about page 47 that Stingo, the narrator who so obviously stood in for my father, lapses into a dream he describes as "the most ferociously erotic hallucination I had ever experienced." On page 48 Stingo elaborates, in extended libidinal detail. "She wiggled toward me, a wanton nymph with moist and parted mouth, and now bending down over my bare belly . . ." If you've read the book, you probably remember this reverie, as well as a host of other raunchy interludes so vivid and numerous that, to this day, I can think of few other literary novels that compare in sheer volume of sexual documentation. If you read the book, you probably laughed. I didn't. I remember leaning against a railing outside the locker room and hoping not to throw up on my Bass Weejuns. *Calm down,* I told myself, furtively delving again into the freshly minted manuscript. *This is fiction. Daddy didn't really DO all these things.*

Well, whatever. He thought them up.

By page 140, mortified and revolted, I had put the galleys back on the kitchen sideboard. I didn't read *Sophie's Choice* all the way through for another twenty-five years.

BY the time I did finally finish what is widely considered my father's masterwork, I was living with my husband and two small children in Vinegar Hill, a peculiar little corner of Brooklyn, and Daddy was dying. My father's last years were an epic, doomed struggle against clinical depression and seemingly limitless physical insults that took advantage of his vulnerable soul. Some stretches were better than others—he rallied long enough to walk me down the aisle at my wedding in 2001—but most of his last half-dozen years were pretty miserable. That they coincided with our move to Brooklyn meant that, among other lost filial pleasures, there wouldn't be many opportunities for us to share experiences of our common hometown.

My father wasn't exactly a hands-on dad. Part of the last generation for whom the Land of Diapers was a mysterious and probably hostile territory, Daddy was also incontestably a Great Male Artist. He not only fit, but helped to create, the cliché of the gifted, hard-drinking, bellicose writer that gave so much of twentieth-century literature a muscular, glamorous aura. All of which pretty much exempted him from parental duties. My father didn't eat dinner with us, attend school plays, or wipe our runny noses. He never threw a ball, built a tree house, or tucked us into bed. I can't remember him teaching me how to do anything except open a wine bottle, a job I did on my tiptoes and with great dedication each night before my bedtime.

Despite all that, he and I had a singular bond. Because I am the youngest of four children by a wide margin, I was sort of an only child. My siblings were all away at school by the time I was seven. My mother, chafing at domestic life in rural Connecticut, had begun a career in human rights work a couple of years before that. There were nannies, but the transition wasn't always seamless. So, sometimes, it was just my father and I. We got along like this: I was a smart aleck, which he liked. But I didn't give him any lip, which would have been disastrous. I grilled my own cheese sandwiches, but I got out of his way when he needed the stove. I came with my homework questions to the door of the living room (where he worked at night, standing at the bar, Mozart blaring), but I let him finish his thought before interrupting. We liked to make each other laugh. We respected each other.

Once in a while, my father picked me up at school. I remember a warm afternoon when I was eight or nine, the sunroof on his old red Mercedes pouring dappled light onto my knees as we looped the gentle curves of Route 199.

"What kind of instrument would a little girl your age play?"

He didn't say so, but I knew his head was in his work and it was for this that he was asking. I didn't have any musical talent but I wanted to be a help.

"I don't know. A piano?"

"No. That's too big. Something you could carry. A violin?"

"Nah," I replied. It seemed boring. Besides, I didn't know anyone who played the violin.

"The flute?"

My friend Lili had a flute.

"Yeah. Maybe," I said.

We didn't speak of it again, nor did I have any idea where a little girl's fancy fit in my father's imagination.

IT was the summer of 2005 when I reread that first line of *Sophie's Choice*, now with an adult's perspective and a pang of recognition. I too had crossed the East River in search of affordable housing. After seventeen years in Manhattan, years that included college and graduate school, I had joined the mighty wave of pilgrims with wedding china in their trunks and buns in the oven. And I too made the mistake, at least once, of confessing the determinants for our move. (I can still feel the chill given off by an indigenous broker when I told him we were looking in Brooklyn because "we couldn't find enough space in The City.")

But in defense of my father, his was a different time entirely. He began writing *Sophie's Choice* in 1973. By then a long-time Connecticut resident and a hugely successful writer, Daddy was a quarter century, a hundred miles, and a world away from the post-war Brooklyn he once knew. The pointy-headed Virginia boy he describes, bobbing in a goulash of *mitteleuropean* immigrants, had aspirations that were quite understandably focused across the river. His literary heroes—Fitzgerald, Wolfe—got drunk at the White Horse, not Farrell's. Even Walt Whitman admired "mast-hemmed Manhattan" from his inimitable ferry. What could young Bill Styron have known of Fuhgeddaboutit Brooklyn Pride? Or the silent fellowship enjoyed by those of us, a generation later, who have *escaped* Manhattan? How could he have understood the surprising pleasure of turning one's back on Gotham and finding that the sun, unobstructed by hulking architecture, falls continually upon you?

To be totally candid, I wasn't quite there myself yet. Oh, I liked Brooklyn okay. And I surely didn't want to move back to Manhattan. But the hydra-headed rodeo ride of marriage and motherhood, combined with some ill-considered real estate choices, had left me exhausted and confused. We had forsaken our first Brooklyn rental, a drafty duplex on Bergen Street, when our loathsome land-lady ignored repeated pleas to address a growing vermin problem. Our second apartment, where I now sat in bed reading *Sophie's Choice,* had mice too. But that, alas, was the least of its problems.

Seduced by an appealing ad in the *New York Times* ("Four bedrooms, European-style elegance, W/D, closets galore"), we had seen the place in Vinegar Hill the day after a magnificent snowstorm. Parking on the quiet cobble-stone street, we checked the number on a tidy brick house before us. Our son wiggled contentedly in his infant seat; the neighborhood glittered under a blanket of white.

"I've always wanted to live over here," my husband, Ed, a knowledgeable urban adventurer, declared with excitement.

As for me, I wasn't even sure where I was exactly. Sleep deprived and pie-eyed on nesting hormones, I only knew that the advertisement, and the cultured Belgian accent of the woman who answered our call, promised to deliver me from the glum parade of "real 2brs!" and light-starved "garden floor-thrus," which we'd seen over the previous weeks. Once inside, the apartment did not disappoint. It *was* lovely, and vastly bigger than anywhere Ed or I had ever lived in New York City. We begged the landlords to take us on the spot, and they did. What is it they say? Never grocery shop when you're hungry? Well, never rent a third-floor walk-up when you're lactating.

It was in pretty short order that life began to reveal what a foolish mistake this particular move had been. Our son started walking but there wasn't, it seemed there on the Edge of Nowhere, any place for him to walk *to*. I got pregnant again. And then the snow melted to reveal— surprise!—we were surrounded on three sides by an enormous power plant, a sprawling housing project, and the tow-pound side of the dubiously renascent Brooklyn Navy Yard. Well, I had *seen* all these features before, but they didn't seem quite so nefarious until I'd been embedded in them for a while. By then it was too late. I was, literally, trapped. Shortly after our daughter was born, Ed began working overseas part-time. And then our dog, a large elderly Labrador, developed trouble climbing all those stairs. My days became a bleakly comic poop-filled dilemma.

I began to dream of the countryside. Of light, and space, and objects found in the natural world my children could learn the names of ("smashed rat," which my son had down cold, not being one of them). When I was single, I'd maintained a mental video of my future offspring, loosed onto a back lawn with acreage and trees and nothing to stop them. The breeze would lift their hair; they would be barefoot and free from worry. It wasn't a re-creation of my own childhood, which, though happier than many, was complex. It was more an idealized version, with all the shadows Photoshopped out. Now, living in Concreteland, that old video became my lodestar. I sent the dog to live in Connecticut and told Ed I wanted to move up there too.

From June of that year well into the following spring, I went real estate crazy. With the aid of a maniacally perky broker whose children had been my schoolmates, I saw dozens of houses for sale in an ever-widening radius and price range. Balmy Summer turned to Russet Fall turned to Christmas in New England turned to Slit-Your-Wrists February (how had I forgotten that season?). The bloom not only fell off the rose, it fell off every living thing in the county, replaced by icy roads and darkness at three p.m. My remarkably agreeable husband became a little less sanguine about the idea of commuting to and from Fargo-on-the-Housatonic. And even I began to entertain frightful visions of loneliness, as well as skepticism about all the wonderful writing I was going to get done with my pre-preschool children nattering at me through the long cold

winter. After disappointing forays down increasingly
unlikely byways, I would return to the house where I grew
up. On his good days, my father was sitting in the living
room, propped like a broken bird keeping warm beneath
the lamplight.

"Hi, Daddy!" I would say as I bounded in. "How are you
doing today?"

"Not very well," came the reply, faint and hoarse.

This was not a surprise. My father's capacity for happi-
ness had pretty much pulled up stakes entirely by then,
taking with it the ability to pretend otherwise. Now his
voice was running off to join them. Like everyone else in
my family, I'd watched my father's decline with a mixture
of disbelief and helplessness, but eventually had learned
to compensate. Unable to solve his predicament, I told
him instead about my own. I talked about the houses and
towns where I'd been, which places looked promising
and especially which ones were truly awful. I edited as
I went, transforming each dispiriting day into a picaresque
adventure, all with the sole intent of raising a smile to
my despairing father's lips. Sometimes I succeeded, and I
always knew he was glad for the company. But in the end,
the irony was hard to escape. This brilliant man, whose rigorous mind had always been intolerant of small talk, now
waited on its arrival, an elixir against his dark and monoto-
nous days.

Every so often, my father asked me about my work.
Respectfully, writer to writer, not expecting much of a

response but interested in whatever I was willing to share. On one of these visits, to pass the time mostly, I told him the plot of my novel-in-progress. He thought it sounded very compelling and I promised to let him read what I had so far. I knew better than to ask the same question of him, and into the silence around us crept the unspoken—his own unfinished manuscript, gathering dust, on the desk upstairs. My father sat in his favorite yellow chair, writing hand atrophied by some mystery plague, mind afield in a pharmaceutical fog. Into the silence too crept all the stories long ago set down.

I sometimes wondered if my father knew I'd never read *Sophie's Choice*. The huge book party, at the River Café (my first trip to Brooklyn), had been a teenage thrill. But it was the release of the film, and the hullabaloo surrounding its success, that truly beguiled me. I saw the movie a dozen times, swept up by the remarkable performances and the melancholy score. In fact, my first and most lastingly powerful impression of the Brooklyn Bridge remains the gorgeous scene Alan Pakula created of Kevin Kline as Nathan leaning out from the cables, champagne bottle in his hand, shouting, "To Stingo!!!" After so much exposure to the story itself, I never felt like picking up the book when finally I was old enough to read it. Then after a while, I felt a little *too* old. How could I consider myself a serious writer and not, in my late thirties already, have read *Sophie's Choice*? How could I be Bill Styron's daughter? How could I live in Brooklyn?

My father had only visited us twice since our move from Manhattan. Once, days after the birth of our son, he came to Bergen Street and held our baby, his namesake, in his hands. He admired our tree-lined street and told me that he had lived nearby, next to a place I'd never heard of, called the Parade Grounds. While my mother, a rich Baltimore girl, always seemed a bit bemused by the modesty of my various New York apartments, Daddy never did. He knew what it was to be making one's way. And, with the exception of the time I totaled the family car, he rarely questioned my judgment at life's big intersections. By the time he came to Brooklyn again, to Vinegar Hill for our son's second birthday, I questioned myself for having invited him. Well into his inevitable unraveling at that point, the visit was an unmitigated fiasco. Even with assistance, he'd nearly fallen backward while coming up the stairs. He then passed the duration of the party in a corner of our sofa, his shock and embarrassment rendering him completely mute. As Ed essentially carried him downstairs at the end of the night, my mother consoled my father.

"Don't worry, sweetheart," she said. "You never have to come here again."

She was right. Six months later Daddy was in the hospital. It was one of the countless stays he endured at the end of his life in every manner of medical facility throughout the northeast. No drug eased his psychic pain for long; no complication spared his body. My father's own curious real estate tour would last another two years, while mine would take me on a different kind of journey entirely.

1506 CATON AVENUE

BROOKLYN 26, N.Y.

JUNE 6, 1949

Dear Pop,

Well, finally summer has come to Brooklyn, after a long period during which it seemed that we'd have winter right into the middle of July . . . the house where I live directly overlooks Prospect Park and often, if I imagine it hard enough, the place seems about as big city-fied as High Point, North Carolina. The street is lined with sycamores and elms, the houses all have green lawns, and sometime—along with the scent of mown grass and burning leaves—I seem not to have ever left Hilton Village . . . it's quite pleasant, if a bit far out from The City itself.

—WS from a letter to his father, William Clark Styron, Sr.

The lone dogwood down our block bloomed. It appeared that spring had come, even to our gritty little slice of the borough. And with the freeze went the last of my resolve for country living. The months we'd spent looking in Connecticut had given me a vicarious experience powerful enough to set my head right and clarify my priorities. Lots of people want to move back home. It just turns out I'm not one of them. Still, I longed for somewhere kinder than where we'd landed. Some place that felt like a small town but, better yet, wasn't.

In the meantime, I began to read *Sophie's Choice*. My excuses for not tackling it before were fair enough. But now I had an almost biological urge to close this gap in my knowledge. I wanted to know my father better and this book, not only its autobiographical content but also what it represented in the scope of his life, would bring me closer to him.

The experience was, well, death-defying. Thrilling and nausea-inducing, dreadful and delightful—not unlike a spin on the Coney Island Cyclone. My father's future and those of his characters became inextricably linked, and I felt the same incipient sorrow as follows Stingo, Nathan, and Sophie on their doomed summer odyssey. As a writer, I tried to figure out how my father kept giving the narrative over so seamlessly to his heroine. (I was amused to discover, in Joan Didion's *The Year of Magical Thinking*, that John Gregory Dunne had passed an entire summer wondering the same thing.) As a new mother, I felt my heart might shatter during the book's eponymous climax. And as a daughter, I wept for little Eva with her "mis," her flute. I wept for myself and all the good-byes still to come.

But something else happened when I read that book, something wonderful in a bittersweet kind of way. I sat in bed at night, the headboard aligned southeasterly, Prospect Park at my back, and I communed with my father in the full bloom of youth. Not Stingo, but Daddy, so vivid and living so close I felt I could turn around and touch him back through the years. Callow, awkward, ambitious, and (yes) horny, his extraordinary life still before him. All his stories yet untold. Each place he named—Flatbush, the St. George Hotel, Williamsburg, the Church Avenue BMT—was like a bread crumb leading me along the map of our common ground. And in the end he gave me a Brooklyn that felt that much more like home.

> *A moveable picnic, our lunchtime repast took place in all of the sunny and shady corners of Prospect Park. I am no longer able to remember how many picnics Sophie and I shared . . . Nor are most of the spots where we sprawled on the grass very clear to me . . . One place however I vividly recall—a grassy peninsula, usually unpeopled at that hour on weekdays, jutting out into the lake where a sextet of large, rather pugnacious-looking swans coasted like gangsters through the reeds . . .*
>
> —FROM CHAPTER SIX OF *Sophie's Choice*

On a crisp April day not long ago, I walked across the park to Caton Avenue. It's no more than a twenty-minute stroll from the house we finally bought in Park Slope to the diamonds of the Parade Grounds. In fact, for a couple more weeks, until the sycamores unfurl their green canopy along our street, I can see my father's old neighborhood from our roof. I left the house with his address and a down-loaded map of what is now called Prospect-Lefferts. The children were playing in the yard and our dog, her twilight days taking her no farther now than the tree out front, lay snoozing on her bed. In the five months since my father died, there haven't been many chances to think just about him.

Sophie had come to him in a dream, he always said. Not much older than I am now, he had awakened in Connecticut and been unable to shake the image of a woman he once knew. She'd lived above him, in the boarding house on Caton Avenue that he would later immortalize as Yetta Zimmerman's Pink Palace. She was a Holocaust survivor, as evidenced by her wrist tattoo, Polish and beautiful, but more than that he didn't know. Her boyfriend was American, but undistinguished. After the book came out, I used to answer the phone at home so my father wouldn't have to. More than once, I remember women with heavy accents explaining the nature of their call in tearful and dramatic tones. *Dad*—my notes would read—*a lady called. I can't spell her name. She says she's Sophie.* And a number somewhere in Michigan, or New Jersey. I never told my father I had read the book. And I never gave him my manuscript either. As I walked through the park I thought about how, even as the clock begins to gong, even when Charon himself arrives, you always think you'll do it tomorrow. You always think there will be more time.

Daddy's Brooklyn house, the Pink Palace, is gone. In its place squats a beige concrete affair, where a Dr. Duddempudi no doubt conducts serious business despite his

Seussian name. Gone too are his neighbors, the "Kingdom of the Jews" (as my father called it), renationalized by colonizers of a more recent vintage. A Jamaican flag flutters from a car antenna, and soccer rules the fields where Sandy Koufax once held his scepter. The "pickle-fragrant air" is redolent of truck exhaust. The food is more fast than kosher. But as I returned to the park, among the cattails that line Prospect Lake, past Concert Grove and Daddy's beloved Mozart, I held fast for a moment to what remained. My father's story, transiting mine, on the green walk home.

BROOKLYN WILDLIFE
Vijay Seshadri

ONE MORNING IN 1987, about eight months after we moved to Carroll Gardens from the Upper West Side, I woke up to my downstairs neighbor yelling, "Shut up, you fucking rooster" from her balcony. I went to bed late and slept heavily in those days. I found myself in dreams that had a brightness and coherence the tenuous waking life I was living—which consisted mostly of trying, and failing, to write poems and feeling regretful about the passage of time (I'd arrived at my early thirties)—couldn't hope to compete with. That morning, not even a rooster could have shaken me from them. My downstairs neighbor, though, had powers roosters lack. She was a moralist; and she was a high-strung moralist—insomniac, quick to spot injustice, one of those people, more common in New York than elsewhere, and more common in Brooklyn than in the rest of the city (why is this?), who find big, grim lessons in little things and opportunities for universal indignation in daily inconveniences and affronts. She was like the primitive car alarms of that era, the Reagan era, activating at the slightest violation of her psychic space, and honking and wailing and sirening ceaselessly. Almost anything set her off—the grinding garbage trucks and their workers, who left our cans strewn halfway down the block; the dog walkers who didn't clean up after their dogs; the glacially paced occupational habits of the clerks at the Red Hook post office; the Fourth of July neighborhood pyrotechnics, which made our streets sound like a war zone; the mourners who double-parked their cars in front of the funeral home on the corner. "The crack in the tea cup opens the lane to the land of the dead," Auden says. Cracks were everywhere in the thin porcelain that protected us from chaos. Even the arrival of a rooster in our densely populated block could be seen not as a mystery and a cause for wonder but as one more opportunity to exercise outraged vigilance, and one more reason to rebuke the world. We were all a little afraid of her.

I rolled from bed, put my pants and shirt on, and went out on the balcony barefoot. There he was, a rooster, on one of the fences separating the backyards below. What was he doing there? He might have been asking the same question. He wasn't crowing lustily, like the roosters in Chaucer and the fables. His crowing was unconvincing and didn't suggest what the word has come to suggest: purpose, enthusiasm, glorification of the self and praise for the day. It was late spring, the sun had been up for hours, the city's intricate labor was well-advanced, but he kept at it in his sporadic way, through the morning, the afternoon, the evening, the night, and into the next day, and the next, while my neighbor yelled and yelled at him. Finally, two municipal workers came with big nets attached to long handles to take him away. He went quietly, sullen and amazed.

The Puerto Rican and Dominican social clubs that ran the length of Smith Street, almost one to a block, have now been mostly replaced by restaurants that have kitchens manned by chefs dreaming of celebrity on the Food Network. In those days, you could walk by and look in a door and see threadbare pool tables, men playing cards or watching *fútbol* on TV, and a *madre de la casa* staring glumly out at the street. I imagined weekly cockfights and heavy betting in those basements, and rooster cages in the paved-over backyards. Had he pecked at his keeper's eyes when he was being taken out to fight and then fluttered away over the walls? I imagined animistic cults in Boerum Hill, from the West Indies, South America, Africa, performing nocturnal rites that had required his sacrifice to appease the powers of darkness. He had escaped the oppression of ancient orders, forms of worship, ways of being, only to find himself washed up in Carroll Gardens, without the will or certainty to take the next step.

So much about the neighborhood was obscure to me in those first years, obscure because I couldn't penetrate it and obscure in itself. It was dominantly black and Hispanic on one side and Sicilian on the other, with pockets of refugees: Lebanese, Jewish, Irish people from the outer boroughs, who were schoolteachers, social workers, anarchist filmmakers; writers and artists from Manhattan; Palestinian families down the street—the women sitting on the stoops in head scarves—who told us they were Yemeni; an expatriate French couple with a shrewd eye for real estate values; Violet, the tiny old Episcopalian lady who lived in a garden apartment and whose ancestors had been in Brooklyn since the beginning of time, inhabiting grand Park Slope brownstones. All of them had satisfied social identities that were beyond a certain point impenetrable, but nevertheless were integral to what the mayor of those days, David Dinkins, called the "gorgeous mosaic" that supposedly is New York.

People looked warily out from their social beings; they were conscious of their borders; they were surrounded by their imbricated ethnic enclaves. The overall tone was Catholic, and the allegiances were working-class. On Good Friday, an effigy of the dead Christ would be carried down the streets leading a brass band playing the funeral march and the sodality of the Church of the Sacred Heart, walking with bent heads. At Christmas, houses all over the neighborhood would be spectacularly attired in Christmas lights, and the carillons in the church steeples would ring out "Jesu, Joy of Man's Desiring." Though the bulk of the shipping industry had long relocated to Jersey, retired longshoremen hung around the two International Longshoremen Workers Union buildings on opposite corners at Union and Court streets—one union offices, the other a clinic—waiting for their pension checks or their doctors. Their children and grandchildren, their nieces and nephews and grandnieces and grandnephews ran the greengrocers and worked in the bakeries.

I didn't find all this gorgeous. I found it bewildering. Having come from America proper (the Midwest and, later, Oregon), having been an immigrant (from India) at a time (the late fifties, sixties, and seventies) when immigrant communities were either nonexistent or incipient in the places I had lived, I had longed to assimilate. I defined myself not by where I came from but by what I did, or wanted to do. And I had come for Manhattan, with its clean lines and verticality, its subordination of identity to ambition, and saw the move to Brooklyn, forced on us by economic necessity, as a kind of defeat. So I was skeptical about the anthropological richness that surrounded me and preferred the animals to the people. The streets and yards were crawling with wild cats, bolder than skunks and fat on a diet of birds and squirrels. There were badger traps in the gardens for them, but they were too clever to be caught. The tomcats sprayed the roses, the mothers deposited their litters under the lilac bushes. We found three kittens under one, and they lived with us for fourteen years. Pigeon fanciers kept coops on the roofs, and you could go up on your own and watch the coveys rising high in unison, spreading out until they were almost dispersed and then collapsing back as if in an invisible purse pulled by purse strings. I was on the sidewalk before dawn one morning, after an unsatisfying night of writing, and I saw, rounding the corner of Court Street and speeding down the block, a pack of wild dogs and had an instant gleam of terror. The moment they noticed me, they crossed the street and loped down toward the Gowanus Canal, where, I was told, they flourished in the shadows of the coffin warehouses and on the embankments by the foul waters. A great blue heron also summered there. At dawn, you could see him flying back and forth.

The heron is still there—he comes back every spring— but the dogs are gone, as are the wild cats and the pigeon fanciers, with their birds. The great real estate storms of the past decade have blown them away, and, New York being what it is, it is unlikely that they will return. The longshoremen's buildings are gone, too—the Church of Jesus Christ of Latter-day Saints has taken over one, and the other is now an ambulatory-care center—and though the cortege of the dead Christ still walks the streets on Good Friday, it is thinning slowly. Almost without my noticing it—or, rather, almost without my being able to register the shifting music through the dense curtain of urban sound and sense—the neighborhood has changed, leaving me with the commonplace but nonetheless sharp recognition that I only began cherishing it when I under- stood it was disappearing. My indignant downstairs neigh- bor moved to Jersey a while ago. In the years before she left, she had three children (and we had one), who sub- dued her and made her resigned, companionable, almost sweet. She was grateful for the help we sometimes gave her, and she and I became good friends. She calls me on my birthday because I share the date with her first son (now in college) and tells me about life in the suburbs, which she hates—they are, she tells me, coming back to Brooklyn to retire. When she called a couple of years ago, I asked her if she remembered the rooster. She said yes, she did.

A CONEY ISLAND OF THE MIND

Katie Roiphe

MY FATHER LEFT Flatbush sixty-five years ago with no intention of ever returning, and one brilliant fall day I find myself going back to deepest Brooklyn, to Coney Island, to the last stop on the F train.

My date stops in front of the Cyclone that curls ominously above us. I am astonished that he wants to ride it. I feel twinges of panic on elevators and airplanes, but it somehow seems too early in our acquaintance for him to know that I am too fragile for roller coasters. My date does not give the impression of being afraid of anything. So we end up at the ticket counter. The ticket seller catches a crazy glint in my eyes and says, "Nothing's happened to anyone in the seven years that I've worked here," and we hear the whoops and shouts and rattle of the cars above us, and I look up at my date and wonder how well I know him.

As we climb into the car it feels rickety. The wooden track rising against the sky reminds me of the dinosaur bones in the American Museum of Natural History, which is not a reassuring image. The other passengers are teenagers from the neighborhood who look as if they do things every day that make the Cyclone about as exciting as a crosstown bus.

Once the ride starts, it does not feel safe. It shakes and moans. This is not the sleek modern sound of speed. This is speed from another era. It's the roller-coaster equivalent of reading by gas lamps or sending telegrams. The Cyclone was built in 1927. "Don't worry," my date tells me. How does he know I am worrying? Am I not doing a good job of hiding my worry? "There's a guy who checks every inch of the track every day." But this is hardly reassuring. This seems to me like a fallibly human system. Why should we trust a man checking a track, a man whose mind could be wandering to his girlfriend's erratic behavior the night before, or what he might be having for lunch?

We are pulled into the sky. I feel as if I am nothing but stomach, air, and fear. As we hurtle to the top, I grasp my bag, my date's legs against mine, and I see the rotating water and sky and sand, the crowd milling below us, and it's the greatest view in the whole city, thrill and terror blending into clarity, panic focusing the mind, I feel like I have never seen the ocean before.

Down below us is the boardwalk where my father used to come with his friends in the early thirties to swim and buy Nathan's Famous hot dogs for a nickel. He rode the cyclone in the brighter, grander, better painted days of its youth. He grew up only a few miles from here, on East Twenty-second Street between Avenue T and Avenue U, in a house that I have never really seen. He drove us there once, on my mother's insistence, but when we got to his block he suddenly put his foot on the gas, and we perceived his childhood house, the house he was evicted from during the Depression, as a blur of color. (Years later, after he dies, I will wish I had gotten him to give me the number of the house; I will wish I had gotten him to talk about the movie theaters where he learned English from Ingrid Bergman, about his parent's marriage, about the Battle of the Somme.) But for now I am a tourist in my father's childhood. I am sailing over the past he wouldn't talk about. I am almost reaching it.

The track dips and the car zips down. My date and I are in our late twenties—he at least seems, ostensibly, to be an adult, but the years are stripped away by wind and fear and we are children again, clutching each other's hands.

It seems as if there is only a small chance that the metal bar will actually hold us in. At any moment we are going to fly out—little dots against the horizon. I imagine us falling through the air, like astronauts in a movie, our hair streaming out in the wind, frozen in a black-and-white photograph the next day in the tabloids.

As we turn the curve, even the teenagers shriek, but I am too scared to scream. It seems as if all of my energy has to be focused on staying alive. In 1911, the Cyclone's predecessor, the Giant Racer, flew off its tracks, killing two women. Picture the tracks bending through the air, the pretty cars careening through the danger they are built to

simulate. Think how long it will take the observers to realize that the screams are real.

It feels as if the earth is falling out from under us and I
have to close my eyes, no matter what my date will think.
We swoop and swerve and finally clatter to a halt. It has
been one hundred seconds.

I wonder woozily why I feel so good. I feel sort of
bruised and banged up but that feeling is part of the beauty
of the Cyclone. It's about terror and the release from terror,
about how close dreams are to nightmares, and how easy it
is to escape from your life. A journalist from the turn of the
century wrote, "Coney Island has a code of conduct all her
own," and for the first time I know exactly what he means.
The Cyclone gives you the feeling that nothing matters but
the second you are in, a feeling worth much more than the
four dollars of the ticket. In fact it may be the platonic
ideal of dates—a whole journey of risk and reassurance
condensed into a minute and a half.

By this point, I am beginning to understand why the city
has always had a romantic fixation on this place. Lawrence
Ferlinghetti wrote his famous poem "A Coney Island of the
Mind" about this too: "There's always complications like
maybe she has no eyes for him or him no eyes for her . . .
or something or other stands in the way like his mother or
her father or someone like that but they go right on trying
to get it all the time like in Shakespeare or Proust remembering his Things Past or wherever and there they all are

struggling toward each other or after each other like those marble maidens on that Grecian Urn or any market street or merry-go-round around and around they go all hunting love and half the hungry time not even knowing just what is really eating them . . ." It's not a happy poem, really, it's not a poem that bodes well, but who remembers anything but the title?

As I step onto what seems like solid ground, I feel light-headed and shaky and my date puts his arm around me. We pass a freak show and a dance contest. We walk on the boardwalk in the warm air. My date is tall and quieter than any other man I have ever met. He does not narrate and analyze his inner life in the same compulsive way as everyone else I know. I look back at the Cyclone, arched against the sky. The brightly painted food stands and arcades bear more of a resemblance to the old peep shows in Times Square than to the glamorous architecture of Coney Island's past. But you can still feel the seediness and greatness of the place, the vague feeling of menace, of leisure and unemployment mixing, along with the elation of a day at the beach.

Four years later, I will marry my date in something of the same spirit as that Cyclone ride. I will be taking a risk that I feel as a risk, and yet it will feel inevitable, as I have bought my ticket and am pulled skyward. Later, when he has moved out, I will go back over time. I will review with some puzzlement what I could have been thinking: Where was that man who checks every inch of the track? What was that man dreaming about when he should have been checking the track?

In Delmore Schwartz's haunting short story "In Dreams Begin Responsibilities," a grown man watches a movie of his parents' courtship. His father wears a tie. His mother wears a hat with feathers. They are trying to impress each other. They ride a streetcar to Coney Island. They ride a merry-go-round, reaching for the brass rings. Then they stand on this same boardwalk, looking out at this same ocean, when his father asks his mother to marry him. Just at that moment the narrator stands up and shouts at this movie screen: "Don't do it. It's not too late to change your minds, both of you. Nothing good will come of it." This is the feeling I have looking at this moment now. Stop the movie, there on the boardwalk. I feel like shouting at myself through the years. But this is what you can't do. *Don't do it. It's not too late to change your mind.*

For now, though, my date buys a large bag of Nathan's French fries, and I wonder how on earth he can eat after what we have just been through, and the crowd is enveloping us with stuffed dogs, and blown-up alligators tucked under their arms, and the sun glistens in the sand, and the sky is as blue as the cotton candy sold by vendors and for now, I am enchanted by the unknown territories of another person, and of the city itself.

RUCKUS FLATBUSH

Jonathan Lethem

THE MANHATTAN BRIDGE is spring-loaded and cars tilt off like bad pinballs aimed with deranged precision at the Williamsburgh Dentist's Bunker Tower and then score, lighting it up with a honking buzz that makes you need your braces tightened again—rubber-band my jaw and start over. Junior's, a Tang wedding cake permanently on fire, smoke and scorch wreathing from the upper banquet hall windows. A guy with teeth the size of manhole covers bites into a cheesecake and pastrami on latkes triple-decker and a chunk of translucent pastrami fat falls sizzling off the curb melting the black tar and causing a swerving wreck between a block-long mafioso stretch limo and a Philip Guston garbage truck with a real dead cat strapped to its grille. Three siblings in identical bowl cuts emerge blinking from the Department of Health, each with freshly fitted Medicare spectacles, identical plastic frames, three Swifty Lazars in Moe haircuts. Mom tugs them across and they get stranded like ducklings on the median line. The wind smashes the hands of the Tower's clock off-line like Dr. Seuss fingers, today is Pluterday, twenty-five o'clock on Ruckus Flatbush!

May not be a crack in everything but there surely is in Brooklyn and you're falling in, scrabbling fingers finding no purchase, help, somebody, I got wedged in Butt Flash Avenue!

Serial killer's picking off the end of the line at the DMV renewal window and nobody notices.

Harry M. Octopus Institute of Practically Nothing Anyhow. One-Year Certificate. One flight up.

WE FIX U GOOD.

Third Degree, Fourth Degree, Butt Flash Extension. South Pockmark Avenue. Corner of Pock and Butt.

Eight-foot tall man in a perfect Malcolm X suit selling whole leopard skins and persimmons oil and cobra venom incense and a table of books by some conspiracy wrangler named Napoleon Fung gets hungry for a Jamaican meat patty wrapped in coco bread. Wrap that in a slice of pizza and cough out a chicken bone you didn't even know was in there. Drumstick bones in an accumulating heap teeter down the subway portal. The city bus skids off Butt Flash, onto Full-Time, doomed pedestrians swept up by its Soylent Green people-catcher depositing them in a jumble onto the Albeit Squalor Mall escalators—going up!

Never Street, Jape Street, Doubtful Place, Murder Avenue. Stifle, between Bums and Hurt.

Soar into space or usc Google Maps to make sense of

this place, read the smashed black orbs of sidewalk gum
like an aerial map of disease vectors, urban dismay, or
merely the exhausted moment when the wrung-out blob of
xylitol spills from your lips. Chew Ennui! Rise higher, now
sight the workmen's gloves scattered in the gutters with
their fat smashed canvas fingers resembling popped corn.
Were their hands lopped off? Higher now, a distribution of
church spires confesses the forgotten plots of acreage and
silence, Brooklyn a planet of towns, plow it up and start
over. Dime Savings Bank was a fieldstone to begin with,
biggest ever. Shifted it out of Manfred Von Bergen's farm.
Metrotech, a meteorite, fell in the '70s, they started scrap-
ing out windows. Plane crashed on Schumer's Horn in '81,
folks were living in it the next day. Yo Mama included!

Turn left on Tightwad. Place you want is on Living
Stoned. Off Smear. Talk to a guy I know. You don't even have
to say my name, he'll know I know you. No, you'll know
when you see him. All taken care of. You talk he talks all talk
no trouble. Cash only! No checks!

This place don't look like much but it's legendary and
nearly historical. They kept slaves on Doubtful Place, so I
heard. Black ones. I remember when they tore down that
theater. They had to close Grim Ugly Plaza because a tidal
wave of rats ran east. Hey, don't take my word for it. You
could look it up or alternately go fuck yourself.

The Aggravated Antic.

Pathetic Street.

Dude snatched a purse and they chased him all the way down Hurt to Why Cough. Dude lived in the Why Cough Garbage.

Guy crawls blinking out of the Lost Isolation Rail Road terminal with a blue Dodgers cap on his head with the visor ripped off, sort of like a Dodgers beanie or yarmulke. White beard down to his scabby knees, covering his crotch, maybe this guy's Rip Van Brooklyn! Nothing covering his ass, though. Hey, Rip, get some pants! That's no Fertile Crescent!

This Times Plaza? Rip asks the nearest passerby.

Thefuckkeryu tokkinbout?

Where is my pawnshop where is my newsstand what's that weird rectangle building full o' gizmos this is not my beautiful intersection go fuck yerself where you been sleeping all this time, old freak? Time don't stand still! Get some pants and cover yer ass!

You ain't seen nothin' yet!

To the Moon, Alice!

Fuggeddabouddit. Gofuckkalamppost. Musteatapileof-shit. Welcome to Brooklyn!

Rip Van Calamity creeps for cover into the Doray Tavern ("Where Good Friends Meet"), a bar like a black hole, day-light bent and broken at its threshold, full of Mohawk ghosts, guys that fell off in-progress skyscrapers chasing a falling half-a-ham-sandwich and ending up embedded to their sternums in Manhattan concrete sidewalks. Here at the Doray they paint the whiskey black. Not the bottles, the whiskey. The ghosts pour shots and chasers down their neck holes and welcome Rip with a hearty hoist of a glass. His kind of people, and he theirs.

Used to work in the then I worked in the that was when I lived in the before all the then after I worked in the then I used to sleep in the before they filled in the hole in the I used to be able to hide in the catch a few zzz's in there sometimes before they filled it all in.

Fuggeddabouddit, Fuggedda, Fugget.

I already Fuggot.

Problem with people these days money. Problem with money these days people. People with money these days problem. People with problem these money days.

The higher you go there you are.

To the moon and all I got was this goddamn parking lot.

Beautiful shadows everywhere.

You like it so much, you live there!

WAS BROOKLYN MINE?
(an author's note)

THIS was a tough assignment for me, and I suppose I took it out on you, dear reader. You see, despite my weird privileged place on Walt Whitman's coattails, I've never had an easy time simply celebrating this borough, this state of mind, this zone of operation, this disputed terrain, this cataclysm of a personal legacy called Brooklyn. Often (for two decades in the center of my life) I strained in the other direction, pulling away from the half-ruined utopian city where I had happened to grow up. I avoided Brooklyn in my life (choosing Manhattan, Vermont, and California instead) and in my work (a failed attempt, as my work always migrated helplessly back, dreaming of Brooklyn on my behalf). For similar reasons, Brooklyn's battles (those battles my parents and their friends, and some of my friends, were often so eager to take up) never seemed my own: I mean, of course, Brooklyn's battles to be reclaimed but not gentrified, to be exalted but not kitschified, and to remain in the hands of the people to whom Brooklyn rightly belonged and not to those "others"—those, you know, carpetbaggers and despoilers. Always easy to spot those when you see them, right?

None of these battles ever seemed to make enough sense to me to take up as my own. Or maybe I was just afraid. Frightened of failure, and of the presumption to speak for such a vast and paradoxical place. I reserved my protective impulse for minute portions, for a single block of Dean Street, for certain irregular rectangles of slate sidewalk, and then even those I cast into a self-questioning nostalgic doubt. Who was I to try to preserve Brooklyn (Breukelen, a "broken land") to begin with? Take Bergen Street, where I lived when I wrote *The Fortress of Solitude*: Did it belong to me, or to the people my parents and their friends half-displaced (So many are still there! As if gentrification was only a veneer over a past that seeps up from underneath), or did Bergen Street belong to the upper-middle-class doctors and lawyers from Manhattan for whom the row houses were originally built? Or to the farmers who occupied those hills before the neighborhood was erected? Or to—? So, better to retreat into doubt. And I did. The Brooklyn I was supposed to have celebrated was always, really, a place that didn't exist except in my vanishing, ambiguous, self-canceling sentiments. As Groucho Marx said, "Hello, I must be going."

Then, recently, with my own neighborhood facing a quite enormous and shockingly bad revision at the hand of politicians and developers, I found I wanted to draw a line in the sand (or if not in sand, then in pavement, approximately at the intersection of Dean Street and Fourth Avenue). This startled me, the commitment I was willing to make to a present-day story, a real battle with stakes outside my fantasia of private meanings. The risk, of seeing wrecked what I'd never completely admitted I wanted to protect, felt vertiginous. As it happened, I'd also just recently quit writing about Brooklyn. I'd reached a limit, for the time being, in the meanings I could plumb from my fantasia. So, this taking-up of a real commitment to the real Brooklyn replaced the writing. Perhaps it was even what the writing had been trying to make possible, all this time. I'd written myself, to my own astonishment, into some long-delayed sense of possession.

And now this. When the request came along from this book's editors, what rose up in me (from the evidence) was a nihilistic fear of suddenly losing what had always seemed so definitively *not mine*. Brooklyn was, possibly, just a fucked place. Wasn't that what I'd proved in my books? It was a Frankenstein's Monster, a monument built by destruction. So maybe it belonged most to the folks who wanted to fuck it up the worst, right now. Not to us natives, but to the barbarians on the horizon. "Ruckus Flatbush," then, is a kiss-off, if you need one. A poison pill. A memo to those who think they can control or define a place like this. Brooklyn: You Break It, You Buy It. Meanwhile, under the looming shadow of such operations, living people and ghosts merely carry on, side by side. Sometimes you can't tell one from the other around here.

ELI MILLER'S SELTZER DELIVERY SERVICE

Emily Barton

FOR MOST OF my life, I was a consumer of bottled seltzer from the supermarket. Store-bought seltzer was what my parents served me when I was growing up, the child of two unaffiliated Jews in suburban New Jersey in the 1970s; it was what I came to like. It was also, importantly, what my father used to make an egg cream, the iconic Brooklyn drink: a little chocolate syrup (traditionally Fox's U-bet, which is made here in Brooklyn, though my father used Bosco, New Jersey's version of Fox's U-bet), a splash of milk, the rest of the glass full of plain seltzer. The milk and soda give an egg cream the froth of a root-beer float, but it isn't so sickeningly sweet; in fact, the seltzer gives it a slightly metallic tang. People are adamant in their opinions about how to make one. My father says the ideal method is to mix a little milk and a dollop of chocolate syrup in the bottom of a glass, then spritz seltzer from a siphon, using high pressure to raise a good head, then ease up on the pressure to fill the glass. This, of course, presumes you have a siphon. We never did, and the egg creams came out fine, but my father assured me the siphon would have made them bubblier. Fox's U-bet's website tells you to put the milk and syrup in the glass, spritz the seltzer onto a spoon in the tilted glass (which also makes a good head), and stir it after. Either way, and probably any other way you make it, it's delicious.

When I was little, egg creams at home were a treat, but they were also a way to tide me over till I could get the perfect egg cream out in the world. (Another such item was a sandwich made with an English muffin, an egg, American cheese, and Taylor ham, much like an Egg McMuffin, but perhaps marginally healthier because my mother had prepared it. This was *treyf* twice over—pork, and meat with cheese—but my parents weren't observant. They sent me to Hebrew school for three weeks in 1976, and when I complained that it was boring, they never made me go back.) I adored my father's egg creams, but I lived for the ones you could get from sidewalk vendors in Manhattan, from silver carts like those that sell hot dogs, undercooked and oversalted pretzels, and, if you're lucky, roasted chestnuts in wintertime. An egg cream and a pretzel rod—the perfect combination, smooth and sweet with salty and crunchy—cost a dime or a quarter in 1980, the kind of money a kid would have in her pocket back in those days when kids sometimes got mugged in broad daylight. And the egg cream you'd get from a vendor was very, very good. It would come in a blue and white waxed paper cup, sort of like a gigantic Dixie cup, whose taste complemented the drink in the same way green glass bottles used to make Coke taste better. As my father had promised, they were frothier than the ones at home, because the vendors made them with a siphon. The bubbles were fresher and springier. I don't know if there's any scientific basis for this observation, but ask anyone who's tried egg creams made both ways; she'll concur.

Although I knew that siphon seltzer was better, it never occurred to me that I could procure it, so I became an avid drinker of the supermarket kind. Sitting with an open bottle—or sometimes two, sequentially—on my desk enlivened the workday, which gives you some idea of how uneventful a writer's day can be. But it got to the point where my husband and I were going through three or four bottles a day—that's a minimum of twenty-one liters a week to schlep home from the supermarket and up the four flights of stairs to our apartment. And we also had to dispose of the empty bottles, either by recycling them or by wrangling them down to the grocery store to collect the deposit, something few people do in this city. It began to seem not only a hassle but embarrassingly quixotic.

But after a time I realized that New York City is one of the last places where you can still get seltzer delivered in those old-fashioned glass siphon bottles, which are beautiful, convenient, and more ecologically sound than plastic because they're washed and refilled again and again. I never saw them in use in my own childhood, but I remember (or imagine remembering) them vividly because I inherited the memory from my father and from others of his generation. At some point in the 1970s, when my father worked in Midtown, he saw a seltzer delivery truck on the street and bargained with the driver to sell him one of the empty siphons, which he eventually got for ten dollars—enough money, at the time, for two full tanks of gas. He still has it in his kitchen. Ask people of his generation who grew up in the New York area about seltzer in their childhoods, and they will wax poetic about the delivery truck, the wooden crates—"the sides were no more than four inches high," my father says, as if amazed that something so small could hold something so beautiful— the glass bottles, which were clear, blue, or green, and the shiny metal siphon heads. My Aunt Edie remembers her grandmother getting seltzer delivered; my father and my Aunt Linda remember the seltzer in blue bottles coming to their own home. (They spent a lot of time with their grandparents, so any of them may have had a blurry under-standing of whose house was whose.) If my grandpar-ents—one from Flatbush, one from the Bronx, one from New Jersey, and one from Yorkville, when it was still home to Russian immigrants—were alive, I bet they could tell stories about their own parents getting soda delivery. My Uncle John recalls that in the 1940s and '50s his family's seltzer was delivered by the Blume Seltzer Company here in Brooklyn; their neighbors in Borough Park owned the company. When his parents were out, he and his sib-lings waged epic battles, spraying each other with the

siphons. This was, of course, also a time when all kinds
of things got delivered: milk, ice for the icebox, eggs,
though my father went down to the local chicken farm
with their empty cardboard box and brought the week's
eggs home himself. Sometimes he'd also have to buy a
chicken, which a worker would kill and pluck for him on
the spot; it would still be warm while he carried it home.
The Fuller Brush man came to your door, as did the Avon
lady, the salesman who offered encyclopedias, and a Bible
salesman, with any luck less creepy than Flannery O'Con-
nor's Manley Pointer.

Though such salespeople are mostly gone, big cities are
the last refuge of their more antiquated trades. Once, in
my twenties, I rode the train to New Haven with my manual typewriter, because the best typewriter repairman on
the East Coast was there. Last year I learned how to set
moveable type and run a letterpress at the Center for Book
Arts in Manhattan, a miraculous loft in which they teach
all the lost arts of bookmaking—flatbed cylinder and
platen press, paper making, bookbinding; the hulking
nineteenth-century machine for cutting paper is called,
charmingly, a guillotine. My neighborhood, like much of
brownstone Brooklyn, still has a guy who drives around in
an old green truck, ringing what sounds like a bicycle bell
to call people from their homes to have their knives sharpened. He usually arrives on a Saturday, and six or seven
of the women on the block will line up with eight-inch
kitchen blades, meat cleavers, and paring knives in their

hands, as if it were normal to stand around chatting with neighbors while holding dangerous implements. He has sharpened my grandmother's desk scissors for me as well as my ice skates. You can still have your laundry washed by hand in Brooklyn, if you're willing to pay for it; and our local cobbler, a Russian immigrant whose gruff exterior belies a sweet personality, can make an exact duplicate of your shoes, if you want him to. So it's no surprise that, given this city's legendary tolerance for the mildly odd and nostalgia for its own past, you can still get seltzer delivery here.

To try to arrange it, I left a message for Walter Backerman, who I knew delivered in Manhattan and the Bronx, asking if he came out here. It was Friday afternoon when I called, and I assumed Backerman was a Jewish name, so I also wished him *Shabbat shalom*, a good Sabbath. My phone call was returned an hour later, not by Walter but by his colleague, Eli Miller, who's been delivering seltzer in Brooklyn for forty-seven years. He arranged to bring by a case the next afternoon, and asked why I'd wished Walter *Shabbat shalom* when my name wasn't Jewish. (When you're Jewish but not a Stein or a Rabinowitz, you keep answers to that on hand, along the lines of "It is a Jewish name, just not one you're familiar with." In my case, I can also remind people that those sticky Almond Kisses that pass for candy at Pesach are made by Barton's Chocolates.)

The next afternoon, Eli drove up—not in the seltzer truck I'd been imagining, the open vehicle with bottles clanking that my father had bequeathed me from his memories, but in an old gray station wagon. He brought the seltzer up the front steps in the four-inch-high crate my father had recalled so fondly; that first delivery, all the bottles were clear, inscribed with the names of the various local factories where they'd been made back when my father was a child. (Our most recent delivery was two cases of cobalt blue bottles, except for one that was dark green and another a pale, soft green, like sea glass. That one, Eli told me, was a safety bottle, completely encased in rubber so I could drop it and it wouldn't break. I didn't try it to see.) Eli is in his seventies, but he's tall and strong, with a friendly smile and the kind of outgoing personality you'd predict for a deliveryman. His accent is pleasantly rough and guttural, part Brooklyn—he was born on Twenty-seventh Street in Coney Island, and grew up in Borough Park—and part Yiddish. (Recently he said to me, "I'm going to see my sister this weekend; she's coming to stay by my brother," a locution my grandparents used, but which now only seems to exist in the camped-up Yiddish world of movies like *The Hebrew Hammer.*) That first time he came, he brought a folder of articles that had been written about him for me to look through, and told me about a children's book, *The Seltzer Man,* that local writer, artist, and teacher Ken Rush had published about him in the 1990s. I ordered the book as soon as I finished hauling the seltzer upstairs—it was only ten bottles, but you have to be a big guy like Eli to carry them all at once. The book's lovely, sun-drenched illustrations in oil are a rhapsody on the vanishing world of seltzer delivery.

Eli grew up in a Conservative Jewish family. His father, Meyer, went to synagogue for all the holidays, and Eli's grandfather owned a butcher shop, so they had a ready supply of kosher meat. Meyer was a housepainter and his wife, May, worked at Ratchik Bakery on Avenue J, but like many families of their generation, they stressed the importance of education, and their children are all highly literate. Eli's older brother became a teacher and an engineer; his younger brother is a computer graphic engineer for Dow Chemical; his sister is a professor at the University of Haifa and has twice been a Fulbright scholar. Eli himself wanted to be a schoolteacher, but when in 1952 he approached his favorite high school teacher, Mr. Hellerbogen, and asked if he should enter the profession, Mr. Hellerbogen said, "Eli, teachers don't make any money at all. You'd be better off driving a truck."

When Eli got out of the service, he went to work on Wall Street. He worked his way up from dividend clerk to cashier, and found himself making $125 a week by 1960— a living wage, but no better than he might have made as a teacher. When he told this to his friend Seymour Kooperman, who drove a soda route, Seymour bragged that he made $300 a week. Eli challenged him to show him how, and Seymour drove him around to prove it. "He was right!" Eli recalls. "There was money in this business."

Not long after, he was sitting around in his cousin Low-

ell Wexler's collision shop on the corner of Ralph and Rem-
sen near Eastern Parkway, wondering what he should do
about his future. "You see that soda shop?" Lowell said,
pointing to the place across the street. "All the black guys
in the neighborhood go in and buy a beer called Copenhagen Castle. You like to sell; you should go get a truck and
sell that beer."

The shop was owned by two brothers, Harry and Jerry
Hittelman. Eli went over and asked about buying maybe
ten cases to start a business in Bedford-Stuyvesant, which
none of the beverage delivery men served. Harry told him
he was crazy to think about going into Bed-Stuy to sell;
there weren't any soda men there for a reason. "Whatever
you do," Eli remembers him saying, "sell for cash. Don't
give credit." Eli bought thirty cases for a total of sixty dollars, which he didn't have on him, but his Uncle Irving
across the street vouched for him. Then he needed a truck.
He found a used van, a black 1949 Chevy, "the old-
fashioned kind, with the two doors that opened in back,"
for $190. Eli's savings, after buying the beer, amounted to
$150, so he went to his mother and asked to borrow forty
dollars. "I don't have it," she said, "but if you need it to go
into business, you could take my silver dollars." Eli didn't
want to take them—many were from the 1870s, and he
knew they were valuable—but he didn't have any other
way to get the money, so he accepted. ("And I still feel bad
about it," he says. "I paid her back tenfold, but those silver
dollars had been special to her.") He paid for the used

truck with $150 in cash and the forty silver dollars, went out with his thirty cases to Bed-Stuy, and sold all of them, half on credit.

When he went back to Harry Hittelman to report his success and buy more, Hittelman said, "You gave those blacks credit on fifteen cases? You'll never see that money." Eli disagreed. "They were honest people," he told him. "They'll be very appreciative that I came around to the neighborhood and trusted them. You'll see." To me he adds, "And wouldn't you know, when I went back the next week, I got every penny."

Eli built up a good route in Bed-Stuy, first with the Copenhagen Castle, which he describes as "similar to a Miller, but less expensive," and later with soda water and the flavored syrups to make Italian sodas. By 1963 he had to sell the van and buy a big clanking seltzer truck like the one my father remembers. But soon after John F. Kennedy was shot, some black kids broke into his truck. When he asked them why, they told him, "We don't want whiteys in our neighborhood," and that they thought the assassination was a white conspiracy. This was an isolated incident; "My customers were good people," he says. "People weren't like that." But soon after Martin Luther King's assassination, a group of young men broke into his truck when it was parked at the corner of Park Place and Bedford, and these kids wanted to fight with him. Eli ran to a nearby drugstore, told the druggist what was going on, and the man came out to the street to defend him. "The drugstore man had been in the neighborhood a long time, and he knew the kids. When he told them he'd turn them in, they ran away." The truck was mostly empty, but Eli felt lucky that no one had been injured. After this, he decided he had to stop working in the neighborhood. When he went around to tell his old customers that he wouldn't be coming anymore, he felt awful. Some offered to come meet him at the curb, so he wouldn't have to come up to their apartments and leave his truck unattended, but it made more sense to move into more middle-class neighborhoods like Bensonhurt and Bay Ridge. Later he also started coming up to Brooklyn Heights and Cobble Hill. Over time, even as business has dwindled, he's also had many customers in Brighton Beach, where there are lots of Russians and older Jews—people who consider seltzer important. He gets his bottles sterilized and refilled by Kenny Gomberg at G & K Beverages in Canarsie, the last seltzer bottler in New York City.

Eli's seltzer is more expensive than the kind we got in the store, so we don't drink it with the same abandon, and the taste is different: saltier, more metallic, sharper. Learning to control the pressure was trickier than we'd expected; we had a few days of wet countertop before we mastered it. Even with soy milk, it makes phenomenal egg creams. But more important, we like having the crates and bottles in our kitchen, a tie to this city's past. I like the connection to my father's childhood, my aunts' and uncle's childhoods, and a world that was based around neighborhoods, where you knew the people who lived next door and ran the shop around the corner. I don't kid myself that Eli is my friend, but I really like him. Not since I was a child and my parents took me to Al at National Shoe Rebuilders so they could have my shoes resoled and I could pet Al's dogs, Lucky and Jenny, and his cat, Snowy, have I so been able to look forward to seeing someone I know so little; and it's a welcome relief in this world in which we do much of our shopping on the Internet, much of our communicating with family and friends on e-mail, to sit on the stoop with Eli and talk politics. He's a lifelong Democrat— a huge supporter of Barack Obama's bid for the Democratic nomination, "though I'm not sure the country is ready for him yet"—and sharp in his critique of the Bush administration. "Eighty percent of Americans want us to get the troops home from Iraq," he says, "and he won't do it. Which makes him a murderer—boys are coming home missing arms, missing legs; more are going to die just because he's pigheaded, not to mention all the Iraqis who are getting killed. And for a trillion dollars! He could have given health care to every man, woman, and child in America for that. He could have given housing to four hundred thousand low-income families. And instead he's going to go down as the most reviled president in our history."

Eli's work life hasn't always been happy; the robberies were small incidents, but one terrible day, his father, who used to help him with deliveries, died on the route. "He'd gone up to visit his favorite customer, an old Argentine lady on Avenue Y and Ocean Parkway. He was up there five o'clock, five fifteen; at five thirty I started to get worried. The super of the building came running out to tell me my father had collapsed on the stairs on the second floor. I tried to revive him, but he was gone. That was the saddest day of my life. Or the second saddest, second after the day my mother died. I was very close to my mother." Despite this, and despite that his job is physically demanding, he takes an overwhelmingly positive view of his work. "This is a hard life," he says, "not an easy vocation. But what has made it wonderful is the people. I deliver seltzer to some of the most beautiful people. And despite the hard work, when you do this, you have independence, no fear of being laid off, and the door is open to work as hard as you want and make as much money as you want. I know it's a little bit of an anachronism, though."

In Ben Katchor's graphic novel *The Jew of New York*, an 1830s seltzer aficionado named Francis Oriole concocts a business plan of tremendous, kooky grandeur: he dreams of carbonating Lake Erie and piping fresh soda water to New York City. Seltzer must have seemed like a miraculous remedy in 1830, and still a relatively novel one—Joseph Priestly, who is credited with stumbling on the happy accident of carbonated water, made his findings known in the 1770s. In Oriole's plan, seltzer would run—or spritz, I suppose—from every tap, and no one would suffer from indigestion. (Many of the book's characters appreciate a good burp, which Katchor refers to by its wonderfully onomatopoeic Yiddish name: *greptz*.) I'm not certain Oriole is Jewish, but he does repeatedly wipe his nose on a "handkerchief embroidered with kabbalistic symbols"; and most of his patrons seem to be Jews, who have long had an affinity for seltzer, I'm guessing because of what many of us traditionally eat. Is there a diet more fat-laden and full of white flour than that of the descendants of shtetl Jews? Though living in New Jersey and not in Minsk, my grandmother fed her three children old-country foods like *gedempft* meat (brisket) and potatoes, latkes, *matzoh brei*, *kuegel*, *kasha varnishkas*, challah with *schmaltz*, and, my father's favorite, *gribbinis*, the burnt fried skin left over after rendering chicken fat. She also kept a vat of oil in the oven and would take it out to deep-fry potatoes for an evening snack. Her house was full of candy—M&M's, Kraft caramels, one-pound Hershey's bars, and Goldenberg's Peanut Chews. I love seltzer, but if I ate like that every day, I'd probably need it to settle my stomach, too.

Eli thinks about seltzer more ecumenically. "The Italians like to mix it with wine or with juices. But people of all faiths and religions like seltzer. At this point, most of my customers are gentiles."

I am generally suspicious of the desire to romanticize one's own childhood—after all, we had few responsibilities then: it was easy to feel the world was benign—as well as of the Luddite tendency to prefer antiquated technologies to those we have today. I still think my manual typewriter is an elegant machine, but it's no match for the ease of the computer on which I'm typing now; and to say that the world was better off without cell phones would be partly true and partly to forget how frustrating it was not to be able to reach someone when you were lost or running late.

When Eli Miller retires, which he hopes to do not long from now, I doubt anyone will take over his route. He's one of only five soda men left in New York City. I'll be surprised if the business exists anywhere in twenty years, when everyone who still remembers it from the 1940s is too old to heft the crates of bottles into their apartments. The siphons will be something I tell my children about, something from another time, the way I know about iceboxes; the Dictaphone; my grandfather's first apartment, here in Brooklyn Heights; and my Uncle David's dental office in Woodside, Queens, so close to the El tracks that his hearing suffered, later in life. I am glad to have experienced this piece of Brooklyn and New York history before it vanishes. Eli is right that his profession is becoming an anachronism; this only makes his seltzer deliveries seem more like a gift.

BROOKLYN PASTORAL

Darcey Steinke

I SPENT A year after my marriage ended looking for a new place for my daughter, Abbie, and me to live. I was hoping to be near Prospect Park. I envisioned taking long restorative walks with my daughter along the leafy pathways. Just when I had about given up, I found a house one block outside Lefferts Gardens, a careworn historic neighborhood across the park from the burnished brownstones and Beaux-Arts mansions of Park Slope.

The house was 120 years old, a small wood Victorian that looked incongruous among the brick apartment buildings. There was something outside of time about it, and, though it was in bad shape, the price was right, cheaper than most studios. After the Realtor had shown the house to me, I walked the five blocks over to Prospect Park, past jerk chicken joints, nail spas, and city buses spewing exhaust. Many of the apartment buildings along Flatbush had broken windows, and a homeless man was sleeping outside the subway station. I wondered if the neighborhood was right for us. Then I entered the park at the

Ocean Avenue entrance through white pillars hung with thick wisteria vines.

It was a Sunday late in April and one of the first warm days of the year. Plumes of smoke rose up into the air as Trinidadian and Hispanic families barbecued by the picnic tables spread out under the trees. I followed the dirt path around the lake, a broad expanse of greenish water surrounded by reeds and willow trees, and noticed the shoreline littered with soda cans and fast-food wrappers but also swans moving in the water, and a blue heron. There was a young Russian couple making out and women in burkas pushing strollers; Hassidic children threw bread out to the ducks. I felt strangely soothed by the scene. The diversity was vast and astounding, everyone moved freely, and yet there was none of the hostility one sometimes sees between people on the subway or in the street.

A few days later, when I took my brother, Jonathan, to see the house, the sky was a ridiculous blue. (As cheap as the house was I couldn't afford it on my own.) At first my brother didn't like the dark first-floor apartment. Though I told him we'd renovate, he was pessimistic. I knew I had to get him over to the park as quickly as I could.

We walked down Parkside Avenue, past the tulips planted at the entrance and across the wide stretch of grass, to the lake. Abbie wanted to ride the paddleboats. We all put on orange life preservers and pedaled our boat, churning up ropes of water. Jonathan was still tentative, quiet and held back from us. Abbie pointed out the turtles

sunning themselves on a log—six turtles, babies resting on
their parents' warm shells. We paddled into a stand of tall
reeds. Inside the narrow passage was a great egret, which
spread its wings and flew up directly over our heads. Under
Terrace Bridge a priest in a black suit and white collar was
fishing. Pigeons cooed in the rafters. We let our boat drift
through the trillions of tiny white petals toward the
Boathouse. The terra-cotta building is based on Saint
Mark's Library in Venice, and when Jonathan saw it I heard
him sigh.

WE moved into the house on Hawthorne Street almost
exactly a year later. My brother, who was half owner, lived
in the downstairs apartment, and Abbie and I took the
upper two floors. I brought Abbie to the park several times
a week to feed the ducks and play along the edge of the
water. We bought bikes and rode them around the loop and
played soccer in a grassy patch near the lake's edge. I'd look
up at the trees, leaves fluttering to reveal their silver undersides. I felt as if my old skin had been burned away, the
new stuff was raw and overly sensitive. I watched the cloud
shadows move over the grass, and dirt began to interest
me. Sometimes on the nights Abbie was with her father
I'd remember the shifting leaves, a dirt clod, the wind-
frenzied branches, and I'd feel comforted.

I'd been dating a man for a few months who was very
much a Manhattan person. He was a wealthy publisher

who frequented the opera, and often sent me home in his private car. Though I'd invited him to the house many times, when Abbie was at her father's house, he'd never slept over. He kept saying he was going to come, but something seemed to always come up. One day while I followed Abbie through the park, he called me on my cell phone. We were just rounding the back of the lake; the wind was wild and enthralling, crazy in the leaves and rough on the water. He was telling me about a writer, someone we both knew, who had just gone into the hospital for Hodgkin's disease. We commiserated, and then I began to describe a stand of iris and an egret, and the sight of Abbie flying down the path in front of me. I could tell by his voice that he wasn't really interested.

Abbie had gotten too far ahead, she was just a blur of gold hair. I called her back to me. The leaves swayed in the wind, a supersize Coke cup knocked gently against the shoreline. The garbage was a constant reminder of the sad parts of my life, how I struggled financially, how no matter how hard I tried to give my daughter stability, nothing I did would diminish the creeping sense of chaos.

I wasn't really desolate after I broke up with the Manhattan man. As he himself pointed out, we hadn't been in love. But I was lonely, still tormented about leaving my marriage. For a long time I had been, I realized, a stranger to myself, numb to the Earth's beauty and my own response to it.

One afternoon I grew so miserable and sick of myself that I fled into the park. I walked around the lake, past the log shelter. At the stand of reeds, children threw scraps of bread to the ducks. I passed the tulip trees and walked down Wellhouse Drive to the path that leads under Terrace Bridge. That first time I was too busy thinking about my tenuous finances and if Abbie was going to pass her next math test to notice the sound of lapping water echoing up against the bridge's steel arches. But the beauty of the myriad leaves and the vividness of the mud along the pathway made me feel I was not in free fall but that I was supported by the Earth. From then on, almost every day after I finished writing, I walked around the lake.

Most days I was melancholy and mired in obsessive thoughts, playing over the time I told my husband we should split up the bank account or the day Abbie told me she didn't want me to leave her daddy. Occasionally, though, I became aware of how the ducks floated gently apart on the lake's surface. It was as if the park and I were moving into a deeper intimacy, things between us were getting serious. After several weeks I started seeing that the tree trunks had different textures; one resembled rivulets of water, another soap bubbles. Leaves, too, were more nuanced than I'd originally perceived, their undersides like the delicate scales of little fish.

I began to feel, at times, that the park was trying to get my attention—that it was trying to communicate with me. I'd see a tree branch sway in a way that was undeniably evocative, or appreciate the preordained and intelligent way a set of trees were arranged. I began to realize that the landscape was constructed to move me, that the park had a depth and integrity nothing like the parks of my childhood—Garst Mill Park in Roanoke, Virginia, where I'd waded in the smelly stream, Patrick Henry Park where I chased my brothers on scorched patches of grass. Though I spent my adolescence living in Roanoke, a town nestled in Virginia's Blue Ridge Mountains, I always found it tedious to hike up Dragon's Tooth or McAfee's Knob. Even at the summit looking out over the pristine mountains I'd feel alienation rather than awe. Prospect Park had meadows, waterfalls, woods— habitats not usually found so close together. It was like massive landscapes had been torn from the greater wilderness, miniaturized and sewn together to make a hallucinatory urban oasis.

More than once when I strayed off paths I knew well, I would get lost. Once over the summer while walking across the park to pick up my daughter at a Park Slope summer camp I went astray in the woods, the last remaining forest in Brooklyn. Chestnut and oak trees soared over my head and while I could hear the traffic on Flatbush, every path I took only led me deeper into confusion. I got so disoriented that I had to call the Audubon Society in the

Boathouse on my cell phone. They directed me to Binnen Bridge. By the time I had my bearings again, I felt flushed and worn out.

At first I blamed the walkways, thinking they were badly marked, but then I realized that their chaotic configuration was intentional. Frederick Law Olmsted, the park designer, wanted me to get lost. Olmsted had designed the park with an understanding of what immersion in nature can do for a melancholy soul.

OLMSTED spent his early years moving from one profession to another. He was a surveyor, a seaman on a merchant ship to China; he farmed on Staten Island and was a correspondent for the *New York Times*, writing mostly about the slave economy of the South. It wasn't until 1857, when Olmsted was thirty-five years old, that he and his partner Calvert Vaux entered the competition for the design of Central Park. Vaux and Olmsted oversaw the construction of the new park, but by 1861 the ongoing political battles over the integrity of the design frustrated Olmsted and he quit. As the Civil War broke out, Olmsted was appointed general secretary to the U.S. Sanitary Commission, overseeing the hygiene of Union hospitals. The job, given the crude medical practices of the time and the heavy casualties, was grim—so grim that near the end of the war Olmsted agreed to run a gold mine in California. Olmsted fell in love with the Yosemite Valley where the mine was located. Soon, though, the mine was in trouble: the owners were embezzling profits and had defaulted on a bank note. Seeing that the mine would fail, Olmsted fell into one of his periodic depressions.

During this time, Vaux wrote him a series of letters asking him to come home to help build Prospect Park. In one letter Vaux drew a crude map at the bottom of his letter, giving a rough outline of the park. On this simple line drawing covered with black script delineating high ground, low ground, and a place for a reservoir, one can see the entrance at the corner of Parkside and Ocean, where nearly every day I enter the park.

Olmsted, who had never been completely happy with Central Park, wrote back to Vaux, "I would like to design a park with a degree of freedom, rather than always accommodating scoundrels." Olmsted realized that the country had been damaged by the Civil War and wanted the new Brooklyn park to be a harmonious place. I understood exactly how he felt.

Built during the 1860s, during Brooklyn's golden era, and covering 585 acres, Prospect Park was the largest single investment made by the city of Brooklyn. When it was completed, Walt Whitman, in one of his columns in the *Brooklyn Eagle*, accused Olmsted of "titivation," and it is true that Olmsted had ideas that sometimes resembled a lush dream landscape. But this, of course, is what makes Prospect Park so transporting: it was first imagined not just as a setting for a patch of grass and some park benches but as an otherworldly utopia.

Many of the park's titivations no longer exist—the Swan Boat Water Carousel, the water display with twenty-four multicolored fountains, the menagerie that featured a bear pit and an elephant house, and, in the exotically named Vale of Cashmere, a seven-sided summer house, a maze, and a croquet lawn, all are gone. More than ornamental flourishes Olmsted was passionate about the landscape itself—building woods, meadows, and the lake to create what is now known as the Olmstedian rush. I feel it as I emerge from Endale Arch. A sensation of darkness and confinement followed by what landscape architects have identified as an opening sense of abundant life.

NOW that I've been living near the park for five years I realize that the dream of a picture-perfect landscape I had when I first moved nearby was an illusion. What I've gotten from being near the park is more challenging than I had imagined, but also more interesting. Maybe it's a mitigated landscape I've always been after, the fireman picnicking beside the lake, the Asian brides and grooms clustering around Lullwater Bridge, an egret stepping expertly around a used condom.

The Parkside Avenue blocks that lead to the park's back entrance are still shabbier than the front Grand Army Plaza entrance in Park Slope. Every time I enter the park I feel like I'm seeing a sort of mirage of leafy trees and shiny lake water. Now when I notice a homeless man in a newspaper hat playing a battery-operated keyboard by the water's edge, I recognize him as a soul not unlike myself, looking in his own eccentric way for regeneration. A robin's nest made with twigs, grass, bits of plastic coffee cups, and shards of cassette tape reminds me that we all make our homes as best we can, with whatever materials are given us.

The other day, walking with my daughter along Lull-water Bridge, we saw a teenage boy in a do-rag and baggy jeans catching turtles. I was afraid he was hurting them, so we walked up closer. He was turning each turtle over and gently examining the creature's yellow undersides before releasing them.

"Aren't they cool?" he asked.

We nodded.

"Want to let this one go?" He handed Abbie a small tur-tle. She squatted down, set it in the lake water, and we watched it paddle its little legs out into the green expanse.

DIAMONDS

Colin Harrison

FEW PEOPLE OUTSIDE my family know that I have a steel, fireproof safe hidden in a downstairs closet in my house in Park Slope. To swing open its heavy door, you punch in a code and turn a wheel that retracts six thick dead bolts. Impressive as it may be, the safe contains no items of monetary value, and were it in fact somehow ransacked by thieves, they would be disappointed to find—in addition to the typical insurance papers and outdated wills—only this: a dirty stack of baseball caps. These eighteen multicolored caps, most scuffed and stained with sweat, are the ones that Walker, my fifteen-year-old son, has worn on all of his various Brooklyn baseball teams. It's no accident they are in the safe—they are precious to me, perhaps as much as any item I own.

Since the age of eight, Walker has played every spring for one baseball team or another; first the "in-house" Little League teams that play only in Prospect Park, then over the last few summers "travel" teams, which play in and around Brooklyn, and now his high school team. (It's become a major undertaking; this year, when you add the school schedule to the travel team schedule, Walker will have played more than one hundred games between March and the end of October.) Every time there is a new cap to add, we take out the whole stack and he fingers each one, recalling aloud the team it came from. Although baseball cards, team photos, old gloves, trophies, championship jackets, practice jerseys, uniforms, cleats, balls, metal and wood bats, helmets, batting gloves, sliding shorts, colored baseball hose, athletic cups, and God knows what else are scattered all over the house, it is the tight stack of baseball caps that I hold sacred. Nearly a foot tall, the stack represents not just the hundreds of games Walker has played over the years, not just my considerable effort to make that experience happen, but something else, as well: our ongoing journey as son and father into the essence of Brooklyn.

NOT many people in Brooklyn, I suspect, know or care about the locations of its many ball fields. Only the players, coaches, parents, and umps. How many fields are there? I don't know. Dozens, anyway, perhaps even a hundred. For starters, the seven fields in Prospect Park, set at the far end of the Long Meadow, a wonder to behold on a spring Saturday when all are in use simultaneously, fourteen teams in their colored uniforms and matching caps out there hitting, running, fielding, cheering. Closer inspection yields the names of the sponsoring organizations across the backs of the jerseys, usually a local business, and the fancy 78 above the brim on each cap, signifying the 78th Precinct, one of the sections of the Police Athletic League. (One year Walker's team had the name of a local bakery, "Faith's Cakes," emblazoned on their backs.) The teams open the season each year with a parade down Seventh Avenue, which the boys find exciting; there they are, a team!

At this level the base paths are sixty feet, the distance from the pitching mound to home plate only forty-five. Parents cluster along the first- and third-base lines talking and watching, often with a baby stroller in tow. But by the time the boys are about eleven they will start watching out for foul balls. In Little League, one first sees the intense dynamic of parent and child and public spectacle. Hope, dream, joy, and fantasy. Some kids are good, some lousy. Some plain awful, either because they never played catch with anyone or just because they have very little eye-hand coordination at that age. From the start, no matter how well-meaning, how "inclusive," the play on the field begins to yield a fateful Darwinian calculus. The good kids find out they are good and the not-so-good kids find that out, too.

As do their parents. In Prospect Park I watched fathers and mothers suppress both their feelings when their sons performed poorly—dropped an easy fly ball, swung at an obvious ball—and when they did well, in order not to appear obnoxiously proud. Much of the relationship between the parents rests on the unspoken rules that one should only compliment another parent's boy and one should avoid bragging about one's own. (Of course the rule is broken constantly.) And yet the parent is also the boy's one unshakable advocate, and the relationship between parents and coaches can become complicated and even ugly, especially as the boys start arriving into their teens and the good ones start playing travel ball—a much higher caliber of game, where playing time really matters. By then, the brutal winnowing of players is well underway, no matter what the parents may want to believe.

(Yes, I'm only using the word *boy* here; there's a very occasional girl playing hardball at the younger levels, but if they keep playing, girls get steered toward softball, and by age thirteen or so have disappeared from the baseball diamond. Which, let me tell you as a father of two girls, seems unarguably right to me, when you see how big some of these boys are and how hard they can throw. By the time Walker was thirteen, I had to firmly insist to him that when we had our tosses in Prospect Park he must not throw his hardest at me; my middle-aged eyes simply can't track a ball that fast, especially one with movement on it.)

Meanwhile, as the boys get older, the number of teams begins to drop and it gets harder to get onto a good one. Walker is a solid player, making a contribution to each team, but usually there have been two or three kids who are better. He knows this, and the lesson is a valuable one: *You have to work for what you get. No one is going to give it to you.*

Walker and I often walked to and from these games, not

a short hike for an eight-year-old boy. We'd toss the ball as we went, dispelling my nervous energy as well as his. In those first few seasons he began to learn the rudiments of the game, and I found myself becoming interested in base-ball as never before. I'd run track in high school and in college and never been much interested in America's past-time. But now, even watching nine-year-olds pitch and hit and field, I began to see what this game really was, as did Walker, and soon we both started to read about the Yan-kees (*not* the Mets) each morning in the summer, listen to their games on the radio and watch them on TV when we could, and of course, go to games. He was so passionate that, at age ten, when it seemed Major League Baseball might go on strike, he wrote a letter of outrage to the op-ed page of the *New York Times*. They printed it, too.

Now, five years gone by, I've learned a good bit more about baseball and at last am beginning to pick up on its subtleties: footwork errors by catchers, late movement on pitches, and even a balk from time to time. My son, mean-while, is a true student of the game. As a catcher, he's now old enough to be calling games, and so he has learned to work the strike zone with the pitchers he's catching, many of whom are throwing in the mid seventies and occasion-ally up near 80 miles per hour—speeds typical of good fifteen-year-olds. The ball is dangerous and I've seen him get hit in the arms, shoulders, chest, legs, neck, and, even though he was wearing a cup, once in the balls, a moment that left him curled in the fetal position in agony at home plate. A kind of rite of passage, this. I resisted running out to him, instead letting his coach go help him—he would have found my presence there embarrassing. When Walker finally stood up, I beckoned him over to the fence, and spoke from experience, having been hit in the balls a few times myself. "You *hurt*, but you are not hurt, right?" Yes, he nodded solemnly. However brief, the exchange was dense with father-son meaning, and, I hoped, reassurance. We're talking testicles here, after all, his future, the family jewels. Within a few minutes, he was okay, and back behind the plate.

If Walker had been seriously injured, that would be another matter, of course, and, as he's a catcher, I do worry about him getting hit by batters, either on the swing or the backswing. Collisions at the plate can be dangerous, too, downright violent. He's a big kid now, getting close to six feet tall, but there are other kids who are bigger and heavier. Just this last weekend we saw a boy who had recently turned fourteen playing for the Bayside Yankees, from Queens, one of the most elite travel programs in the country. The kid was six three and two hundred pounds. He hit a homer—or as it's known, a *shot*.

ONCE a boy is on a travel team, many of which play not only in Long Island, Queens, and Staten Island, but also in tournaments up and down the Eastern seaboard, players and their parents start dreaming about college scholarships, getting into the minor leagues, or even, yes, getting that mystical bid at the majors. No matter the statistical absurdity of such a notion, there are fathers who dream this for their sons, perhaps because they know, deep within themselves, that their ability to project their sons forward into the world is quite limited. The dream becomes the thing that solves both the insufficient past and the risky future and it is protected at all costs. There is a certain kind of father who presents himself before the game as an affable yet knowledgeable bystander but who has begun to chew at the coach or ump or even his own son by the second inning. These are the fathers who yank their kids from team to team, who form cabals with other parents to undermine a coach, who seem intent on being a player in the game outside the game itself.

There are also the fathers who tell themselves that they are being realistic about their sons' chances of making the majors, who throw around terms like *statistical absurdity* as if that proves anything, and who yet, privately, have been known to wonder what it would be like to watch one's broad-shouldered son trot gloriously onto the sun-drenched field of Yankee Stadium. Yes, there are fathers like that, and I know one quite well.

TO get to his travel games, Walker and I have to leave the house long before the game begins, getting up early to load the minivan with the equipment, the huge colored bottles of Gatorade, and, for me, a folding canvas spectator chair. The earlier you leave, the better, especially when the weather is good and people want to go to the beach. There are the many clusters of diamonds along Brooklyn's Belt Parkway, and they should be enumerated here because they are important—a secret organ in the functioning of the borough during the summer. First are the fields on Shore Road, where you can turn around from the game and spy the enormous red-hulled container ships pushing up into New York Harbor; then at Exit 4 the various Dyker Beach Park fields, where as soon as the sun is up you encounter young Mexican men playing soccer, Chinese guys playing hoops, and old Italian men chewing unlit cigars playing boccie. (If the Mexicans don't leave quickly, there's often a brusque conversation about who has "the permit.") Across the street from the northeast corner of Dyker Park is the building that used to house the 19th Hole, a notorious mafia hangout in the 1980s; a lot of murders were ordered there. On my way to buy bagels with cream cheese in between double-header games, I've lingered on the sidewalk outside this building, secretly thrilled, and wondering if any of the old Italian guys playing bocchi nearby were ever inside the 19th Hole back in the day. But it's not like I can ask. This is Brooklyn, yo.

Also at Dyker are the three beautiful Bay Eighth fields, their brick bleachers shaded by oak trees. This is the home of the Kiwanis League, and the man who controls it patrols his empire on a battery-powered three-wheeled scooter, going field to field to adjust game start times and to check if the umps have arrived. (I once picked up six baseballs in the high grass along one of the left field lines there, gave three to Walker's team, the purple-capped Bensonhurst Rams, and kept three for him.) Then, looping around Cropsey Avenue as it hits the beginning of Seventh Avenue you see the spotless Poly Prep School field, where the home team plays Berkeley Carroll, Collegiate, Long Island Lutheran, Hackley, Trinity, and other New York City schools. Walker has played here, too.

Back on the Belt Parkway, the next fields can be found at Exit 5, the Benson fields, where the diamonds are not twenty feet from the lapping water, and the Belt is so close to the outfield that a giant homer will bounce into the eastbound lane of traffic. Last summer, as my son played on this field, some of the neighborhood girls—fourteen- and fifteen-year-olds in tank tops and short shorts—showed up at the game to check out the young ballplayers. They made themselves so conspicuous that the coach had to tell them to knock it off, to stop flirting with his ballplayers. They sulked a bit, popped their gum, but didn't leave. Abashed at the whole thing, my son smiled, his mouth full of braces.

Exit 6 gives you the "Six Diamonds" fields, also next to the water, but keep going east on the Belt. Get off at Exit 11 south. I'm going to count the five fields at Fort Tilden at Breezy Point in Rockaway as part of Brooklyn, since the Kings County (Brooklyn) line is a few hundred yards from home plate and most of the boys who now play on the home team there, the Sea Dawgs, are from Brooklyn—including number 16, my son. They have very cool blue and white uniforms, and a fabulous hat with the Sea Dawg emblem—a cartoon figure of what looks like a seal with the head of a boxer. (The cap is *so* going in the vault at the end of the summer.) Breezy Point also is the Berkeley Carroll School's home field. Both the Sea Dawgs and Berkeley Carroll are superbly coached by Walter Paller, a well-known, longtime figure in the interconnected world of Brooklyn baseball (and I'm not just saying that because he's my son's coach—ask around). The players bus there from Park Slope five days a week all through the spring, and try to avoid the copious droppings deposited by the Canada geese. To get there, you turn into the old fort and pass a barracks converted to a clubhouse for the kids. The other barracks were burned down to make way for the ball fields. The long-timers there credit Senator Charles Schumer, then a Brooklyn congressman, for helping to get the fields built.

For a small independent school Berkeley Carroll generally has very good teams and often makes it to the state playoffs. Its most famous player is Adam Ottavino, a six foot five right-handed pitcher who graduated in 2003, was drafted in the thirtieth round by the Tampa Bay Devil Rays, and went to Northeastern for three years, where he developed so much that he was subsequently drafted in the first round of the 2006 draft by the St. Louis Cardinals; he now plays Class A ball in the Cardinals' farm system, and his major-league prospects are excellent. Every kid on the BC team knows about him.

They also know—as does every ballplayer in Brooklyn—about the borough's most recent phenom, Dellin Betances, a six foot nine hurler who threw the ball in the high nineties for Grand Street Campus, and was drafted by the Yankees in 2006. My son, away on his eighth-grade overnight trip, missed the chance to be among the other Berkeley Carroll players as they watched Betances hit a four-hundred-foot homerun.

BACK on the Belt, get off at Exit 13, where, tucked away beneath the flight path of JFK, are the three operational and one abandoned American Legion fields. The jumbo jets float overhead so slowly they look like they can't be flying. One passes by every minute or so, just high enough to be soundless. At field level, the snack bar is in the center of the complex and sells pretty good soft pretzels. The men's room, on the other hand, is littered with sunflower shells, especially in and around the urinal. The Latino fans coming to games at American Legion, especially fans of the much feared and legendary Youth Services teams, are known to use air horns. The Youth Services players sometimes sing songs inside the concrete-walled dugouts. Manny Ramirez, of the Boston Red Sox, is the most famous player to come through the Youth Services program, which plays all over the city. A few summers ago, Walker filled in

on a thirteen-and-under Youth Services team for a couple
of games. The team had just lost a lot of players and they
needed boys. We gave back the uniform, but the two
caps—a blue and gold job with a yellow lightning bolt and
a white one with THUNDER embroidered in blue on the
back—are now in the safe. They're special.

In nearby Bergen Beach, the fields are tucked away at the
edge of a marsh. Walk miraculously over the brackish waters
of Fresh Creek Basin, push your way through the high grass,
and you'll encounter more ball fields. Decades ago, somebody in Brooklyn figured out that you can put baseball
fields where nothing else can go, and make a lot of boys
happy that way—and maybe keep them out of trouble, too.

Let's work our way back into the heart of Brooklyn.
There's the St. A's field on Fifty-third between Twenty-first
and Twenty-second, a private one with a nice little clubhouse tucked away to one side and a very short left-field
wall; at a father-son game there, I pulled my groin muscle
so badly chasing a fly ball that it looked like someone had
taken me down with a rifle shot. I limped off the field,
much to the embarrassment of my son. Not far away are
the crummy, overused fields at the park at Fifty-eighth
and Eighteenth avenues; the asphalt yard at Hamilton
Parkway and Seventy-seventh Street, where the Bensonhurst Rams hold tryouts in the morning of Super Bowl
Sunday, weather permitting. Heading east there are about
six so-so fields in Marine Park, weedy and a bit lumpy, and
a few blocks away is the sweet little park called Amity,

tucked away behind a wall on Gerritsen Avenue. This is where Walker played when he filled in for the Youth Services team. He was nervous and so was I. On his first chance he snagged a fly ball in right field and fired it home. Thrilled? Yes, I was. And even more so when he clanked a ball deep to left on his first at bat.

WHATEVER happens, we talk about it afterward on the drive home. We discuss the ump, the other team, the pitching, and Walker's at-bats. Maybe some close plays. What happened on errors—whether the mistake was physical or mental. If the day was a doubleheader (or a triple header or even, once, a quadruple header) and it's now late in the day, with the Yankees game over, Walker often takes off his shockingly odorous baseball shoes and sprawls asleep in the front seat, able to be woken only if I pull into one of the McDonald's along Fourth Avenue. I have to remind him not to hand me my hamburger while I am trying to pull into traffic. Then the game talk will resume. I find our analysis intensely pleasurable, because I know the players, their tendencies and abilities, but all the more so because I can see Walker's intelligence and perspective continuing to deepen. These games, these summers, are adding up to a profound experience, one he will take with him into the decades to come.

If he plays during the week, and has caught a ride with a friend, I hurry from my air-conditioned office in Rockefeller

Center, rush home on the B train, jump in my car, and suddenly I'm a world away, bouncing over the moon-craters of Flatbush Avenue in a desperate attempt to catch the last inning or two. If I do not make it to the game I can nonetheless tell how it went as soon as Walker comes in the front door dragging his enormous equipment bag. Either he's disgusted and noncommunicative, or else he will casually announce, "So, uh, Dad, we won, I went two-for-four with a ribbie double over the second baseman." Or some such. Much of the pleasure of watching and knowing baseball is to live within its particular lexicon, its secret language.

HEADING back toward Park Slope now, I realize I've forgotten the fields on the Parade Grounds on the other side of Prospect Park. These are always crowded. Before they were repaired a few years back, Walker took a bad-hopping grounder right in the eye there; I bought ice at a bodega on the way home but his shiner was so bad that I took a photo of it for posterity. There are the bumpy fields of Red Hook Park; just west of the Brooklyn-Queens Expressway is the tiny field at the Vincent Dimattina Playground at Hicks and Rapelye streets, where just beyond the right field wall apartment windows look down upon the grass; also next to the BQE, in Brooklyn Heights, is the manicured little field on Vine Street; and, jumping across the borough to Avenue X, off Stillwell Avenue, are the two diamonds of Jim Franco Field. A Google satellite photo reveals how small and

nearly off kilter they are. There's too much trash and broken glass in the weeds there but the snack bar is excellent.
Behind the fields rise the elevated tracks of the MTA facil-
ities; the subway's yellow service engines sometimes sit up
there, and once I heard the engineer blast his horn when a
boy hit one to the wall. I have a special feeling for this park;
I think it's where my son hit his first baseball in a game outside Prospect Park, a high outside pitch, way over his nine-
year-old head. He was so excited he just swung at the first
pitch he saw. He batted about .600 that season, which you
can do if you are nine. On summer evenings, teams playing
there will, after the game, drive over a few blocks to one of
the large outdoor pizza and spaghetti joints, sit at the picnic tables under the red and white flags, and gorge on
everything—the fried shrimp, the onion rings, the calzone.

I know I am forgetting fields where I've only been once
or twice, as well as the many fields I've never seen. But any
listing of Brooklyn ball parks must include the best field in
the entire borough, the minor league Keyspan Park in
Coney Island, home of the Brooklyn Cyclones. Under the
bright lights the field there is *perfect*, table-flat and a vivid
green, with the ocean misting away into the blue dusk out
over the right field wall. Walker has played there, too, for
his high school team. I'm sorry I missed it.

HOW do I know where all these Brooklyn fields are? I've
learned the hard way, getting lost, asking directions, figuring

it out. On the battered and repeatedly repaired pages of my Hagstrom's *New York City 5 Borough Atlas* I've actually drawn in the diamonds on the unmarked parks and lots where they sit. And, of course, I have Google mapped my way all over Brooklyn, to locate the fields, then found myself switching to the satellite photo feature to be sure there really was a field where I'd been told there's one.

Just getting to the games has been an education for us. We've zigzagged all through the heart of Brooklyn. Flatbush. Church Avenue. McDonald. Bay Parkway. Ocean Avenue. Ocean *Parkway*. Coney Island Avenue. Nostrand Avenue. Shore Road. We see people, situations, the street, the delis, bodegas, pizzerias, car services, garages, nail salons, churches, the police cars, the people hanging on the street. The whole thing, the *Brooklyn* thing, playing out before our eyes.

But it's at the games themselves that the pressure and yearning and energy of Brooklyn seem most manifest. The parents and players and coaches make a huge effort to make the competition happen. They wash the uniforms out the night before (in a pinch, you can do this in the bathtub with Cascade dishwasher powder, I've learned, making the dirt seemingly explode off the uniform), they've found the cleats, gotten the boy up early (I make Walker two fried eggs on weekend mornings), driven to the game, scheduled the game with the other team, arranged for the umps, secured the field. Then comes the dusty, hot, and sweaty enterprise itself. It's hard and takes effort. It has to come from deep within. You have to love the game but also love the grandeur of the attempt to play it well. And hey, a lot gets worked out among the players, parents, coaches, and umps. Father-son stuff. Racial stuff. Class and education differences. Talent differences. The problem of tribes. I will not go so far as to say that this is essentially different from what is worked out in ball fields all over America, but I believe it has a Brooklyn cast to it; the populations are so diverse, the attitude of the street is literally next door, and the emotions often run high. If the American game is to be played to its conclusion, differences need to be overcome, rules need to be observed.

My son sees and feels all this; it's going into him, along with the Gatorade, as he listens to the coach call out the batting order and player positions. The team claps and yells with each name. Walker trots out onto the field with his mask and glove and chest protector and takes the first warm-ups from the pitcher. This is the moment I love most. When it's starting. You don't know what is going to happen, but it could be good. The days and years are passing quickly; the time is now, the game is now. The ump is dusting off home plate, the batter stepping into the box, his face all business. The infielders bend over in expectation. The coach claps, says let's go now. The pitcher looks at Walker, waits, see the fingers of Walker's right hand flashing the sign between his thighs, then nods when he gets it and adjusts his grip on the ball within the secret recess of his glove. Walker settles lower on his haunches, sets the mitt where the pitch should arrive. The batter freezes with bat poised. Here's the windup. I'm there, hanging on the moment, my fingers curled through the chain-link fence, witnessing my son's Brooklyn boyhood, lived through baseball.

MAKE A LIGHT

Philip Dray

I GREW UP in amber-waves-of-grain America, more than fifteen hundred miles west of New York City, but it was in Brooklyn that I learned what it meant to live in a small town.

When my wife, Lianne, and I arrived in 1988, Northside Williamsburg, just across the East River from Manhattan, had one stoplight, a "town drunk" named Angie known for lowering his trousers and lying down in the middle of Bedford Avenue (our "Main Street"), and a store that sold pickles. It was so sleepy a place that if you weren't in a seat at Kasia's Polish Café by 8 p.m. you could forget about eating dinner. From our windows we'd see people running to make it before the kitchen closed.

Williamsburg has an almost bottomless past. There's an old vaudeville theater on Metropolitan and Driggs where a neighborhood girl named Mae West performed; now it's a warehouse for marble and Formica tabletops. The author Henry Miller's childhood home across the street is something of a local landmark. Funny to think those two might have known each other. McCarren Park, which divides Williamsburg from adjoining Greenpoint, was once a watery inlet from the East River; along its banks, we're told, seasonal gang battles were fought between rowdies calling themselves "Pointers" and "Burgers." During a little-known incident of the Revolutionary War, Americans opened fire with cannon from the Brooklyn shore on a British frigate in the river, killing a cow.

By the nineteenth century Williamsburg had become a shipbuilding mecca (the Civil War ironclad USS *Monitor* was launched from an inlet at the end of North Thirteenth Street); Domino Sugar and Pfizer opened large refining and manufacturing plants; breweries, metal stamping and fish-processing factories followed, as did, more recently, artists, writers like me, and musicians like Lianne, drawn by the space, the quiet, and the cheap rent.

Today, the area is rapidly losing its working-class, bohemian flavor and becoming a cookie-cutter bedroom community for Manhattan, its sepia past closing like the iris dissolve at the end of a silent film.

Vanished are the candy stores with the wooden phone booths; Joe's "Busy" Corner Deli, with its gracious sign: "You Ring, We Bring"; the "hillbilly" family who ran the Laundromat on Bedford and North Eighth; tiny neighborhood social clubs like the Bog and Quiet Life, where They Might Be Giants, Laura Cantrell, and Lucinda Williams once held forth.

"We made it too chic around here," Lianne says ruefully,

as we stroll by another high-rise development. "Blame the *New York Times* Style section," says me. "They're the ones who couldn't keep a secret."

Actually, I suspected the end was at hand back in 1995, when a German tourist asked me for directions to the Salvation Army Thrift Store on Bedford and North Seventh Street, then showed me several pages describing Northside Williamsburg in her *Lonely Planet* guide. No neighborhood can survive that.

Barely remembered today is the original, hole-in-the-wall Planet Thailand, granddaddy to the huge Asian theme restaurants that dominate the neighborhood today, its prospects then so humble the menu offered, just to be safe, hot dogs and grilled cheese sandwiches.

No more do our neighbors keep rooftop pigeon coops or do the pet shops sell "food for hoopoes"; nor do Polish daylaborers huddle together for warmth on the corner at dawn, cradling the day's first Budweiser.

Gone are the wiseguys who used to gather in the window at Teddy's Bar and Grill each Sunday morning, poring over the sports pages to scope out the football odds.

Exiled to nearby Greenpoint (fuggedaboutit!) are Charlie and his partner Sabby of S & G Auto, who would fix your car . . . sort of.

As in any small town, however, some cherished features remain, refusing to go quietly. Such is the case with our octogenarian landlady, Milli. You might have seen her—a sturdy five feet, three inches in her fur Cossack hat—chasing discarded pizza plates and other litter from our sidewalk, or sweeping latte-bearing NYU students off the front stoop. Whether you're a student or a pizza plate, she will take a broom to you.

Indoors she's equally rigorous, each Friday night Lemon Pledge—ing the entire three-story wood-paneled stairway on her hands and knees. (The exertion, or the fumes, would have long ago killed a lesser woman.) Meanwhile, her war of extermination against our building's "cock-o-roaches" has been so thorough, I wouldn't be surprised to see her someday brought up on charges at The Hague.

A formidable link to the neighborhood's past, Milli is also a staunch defender of its traditional values:

Husbands shouldn't buy groceries.

Parking meters are not bicycle racks.

It's unsafe to sit in the sunlight and eat a sandwich made with mayonnaise.

During a terrorist attack (we learned this as the twin towers collapsed on 9/11) you *still* remember to put out some babka.

Who needs to hire some fancy electrician? Bah! An arm and a leg it will cost me. Mr. Duda was handyman in Warsaw. He can fix.

Without God in your life it's Satan who steps in, and if there is no God, *smart guy*, who else put the moon and stars in the sky?

"Make a light," she says each evening when she hears

me climbing the darkened stairs. For nineteen years I have made a light.

"Kalt today!" she announces. Yes, I agree, very cold.

"Put by the curb," she commands, seeing me headed downstairs with the trash. Milli, where else would I put it?

"And close the curtains upstairs, across the street they'll say it's gypsies here."

She asks sincerely, "Why do you go to New York all the time, you don't like it here?" We like it fine, I explain. (To Milli, Manhattan is "New York.")

"That goddamn Bush!" she declares. Yes, we say, goddamn him. "Okay then, Philip," says Milli, "make a light."

MILLI'S concern about what the neighbors might think is not all that misplaced. This is a small town, and we all know one another's history. Milli, it so happens, relates her own life story with considerable pride (and for any parts she leaves out you can rely on Mrs. Zbignei over at Koskiuszko Florists).

Milli was born to immigrant parents in Brooklyn in the 1920s but was reared by relations in Europe, her parents believing America no place to raise a traditional Ukrainian girl. Returning on the eve of the Second World War, she found work as a "Rosie the Riveter" at an airplane factory on Long Island, and soon met and married her Polish husband, Peter. His job was in the distant Bronx, to which he traveled each day by subway, while she joined the night-shift at the Williamsburg Pfizer plant. ("Thank God for the Pfizer!" she likes to pronounce, the firm having been generous to its many neighborhood retirees over the years.) They settled at first on Metropolitan Avenue and had a son, Michael (today one of Northside's community activists), before in 1969 buying our building on Bedford Avenue for $20,000, a tiny fraction of its current value.

One day in the 1970s, out of a clear blue sky, she received an urgent call from her husband's work: Peter had fallen down by some machinery. She rushed to the Bronx to learn that he had died at the hospital: a massive heart attack. His sudden death—he was in his late forties—was a shock from which Milli never fully recovered, leaving her suspicious and jittery about unexpected occurrences (when she's feeling vulnerable, a packet of Chinese menus left in our ground-floor mail slot becomes a potential letter bomb). Resisting the blandishments of several Polish and Ukrainian gentlemen who sought her hand, she brought Mikey up by herself and, after he married a neighborhood girl, helped raise her two granddaughters, Cheryl and Julie.

Milli and her husband used to spend summer weekends at a Polish family retreat in the Catskills ("Agggh!" recalls Milli, with her distinct blend of rage and tender sentiment, "where I'd *cook* and *cook* and *cook*.") They were so fond of the area she buried Peter up there, near pastoral Monroe, New York, and for years she regularly visited his grave, although recently she's found the journey too difficult.

She still attends Mass each Sunday morning with Mikey and his family. After lunch she peruses the *Daily News,* and in the afternoon works in her small backyard garden, trimming the roses and nurturing her small vegetable crop; we thank her for the cucumbers she leaves on the stairs, but never eat them, given that the neighborhood sits atop a massive underground oil spill, a haunting legacy of the community's industrial past.

Milli may not care much about the subterranean environment but she's an encyclopedia of what's gone on aboveground. Mention a name, a business, or even a street corner, and she'll sigh, take a deep breath, and serve up the history. These stories all seem to share a common arc—a person of her acquaintance who, although attractive, well-off, or otherwise fortunate, did something foolish out of greed, lust, or ignorance, and paid for their mistake by losing the respect of the community. The result, typically, was self-banishment—to Florida, back to Poland, in the worst cases to Long Island, a fate Brooklynites equate with oblivion.

Milli herself has carefully heeded the moral of these tales, nurturing her connections to the neighborhood and the people close to her. Each New Year's Day she invites the priest and choir members from her church to come and bless her apartment with prayers and song. Summer evenings you'll find her settled in a lawn chair on the sidewalk, chatting with old Ukie or Polish friends or the Arab grocers from across the street. Once, seeing me carry a duffel bag toward the subway for a weekend trip, she ran halfway down the block holding a large packet of tinfoil, out of breath and indignant that I'd leave town without some kielbasa.

As landlady and tenants living on top of each other, we long ago achieved peaceful coexistence with Milli. She pretends not to hear my wife's electric guitar late at night; we, in turn, never mention that, as her hearing's diminished, her TV's gotten louder.

But there have been occasional rough spots. Once, coming home at 2 a.m. with a bulky instrument bag after a gig, Lianne inadvertently knocked over a plastic vase with plastic flowers in it that Milli keeps in a wall niche on the landing. To us, the vase had always seemed like something from a tag sale. But to Milli, who we heard shriek when she found it on the floor the next morning, this was a desecration, one that pained her in a way we never fully understood, and for which we were never able to adequately apologize.

At such times she seems so innocent, as when she worries that "yuppies" are encroaching so quickly on the neighborhood they are already living in the half-built luxury condo tower down the block; I point out that yuppies don't wear hardhats, those are construction workers. But she's neither a fool nor a pushover. Like others of her generation she marvels at the changes in our neighborhood, and knows what they mean for property values; her friends, many of whom also own houses, taunt her with tales of the sky-high rents they are collecting from new arrivals. Nor is she above tactlessly reminding us of these trends, when her arthritis flares up and puts her in a sour mood, or when she sees we've ignored (again) her edict to remove our window-boxes from the fire escape.

"Milli," we say, "why would you want strangers in your house, when you can have us?" Always at her most lucid when the subject is money, she waves such sentiment away. "Listen, you don't know . . . to manage a building in Brooklyn . . . it's plenty."

She's right, after all. The cooped pigeons and candy stores have vanished from Northside Williamsburg, memories don't pay the bills, and she could use the added income of a higher-paying tenant. Someday, maybe soon, Milli will want to go her way, and we'll have to go ours. The pressures on everyone are simply too great.

In the meantime, we'll cling to our perch, fiercely attached to our home of nineteen years and yet, like so much else around here these days, at risk of becoming extinct.

BRIDGES

Joanna Hershon

IN THE EARLY part of the twentieth century, a Jewish girl from Poland, in the United States only weeks, went to a dinner party in Brooklyn. As she entered the house, a young man was putting on his coat to leave. When he saw the young woman coming through the door, he promptly removed his coat. Before the end of the night, he asked her to take a walk on the Brooklyn Bridge, and she accepted. As they stood together, overlooking the wide expanse of Manhattan and Brooklyn and the East River, he proposed marriage. She accepted that too.

DO *you remember the story of your parents' meeting and getting engaged?* I ask my ninety-two-year-old grandmother, recently. She doesn't remember where I live or how old I am, but sometimes she can reach the most distant corridors of memory, so I try.

No . . . , she says. *You know, I have trouble remembering.*

My grandmother was never the greatest of storytellers,

but she had, until recently, possessed an admirable enthusiasm for the telling.

There was a story you told us, I cheat, I lead; *your father
asked your mother to take a walk on the Brooklyn Bridge and
he proposed?*

Really?

Well, it's what you told us.

My, she says, *what a marvelous story.*

WHEN it was completed in 1883, the Brooklyn Bridge
was declared the longest suspension bridge in the world.
But, as David McCullough writes in his masterful 1972
book *The Great Bridge*, it was the "future impact of such a
structure on their own lives that interested people most."
The bridge promised relief from the overcrowding and
crime of New York, convenience for Long Island farmers,
Brooklyn brewers and—most appealingly for the com-
muter crowd—a safe and reliable alternative to the East
River ferries, which were notoriously affected by gales and
frozen water. Expectations were so heightened it soon
became clear that this bridge was to be much more than a
magnificent achievement of engineering; it was to be—like
the transcontinental railroad or the Suez Canal—a symbol
of a new age.

The elegance of the end result belied a famously cursed
evolution. At fifteen million dollars and fourteen years (not
to mention the loss of at least twenty lives), it cost more

than twice as much and took nearly three times as long as the chief engineer, John Roebling, had estimated. Before construction even began, Mr. Roebling died from tetanus, and, shortly after his son, Washington Roebling, became his successor, he was plagued by "the bends," a crippling illness we now know was a result of working underwater in the caissons used to sink foundations into the riverbed. Determined to continue overseeing the project, Washington kept watch over the bridge's progress from the bedroom window of his house on Columbia Street in Brooklyn Heights.

But the bridge's construction is also steeped in a romance of sorts, or at least in the bedrock of marriage. As he directed the action from home, Washington was fortunate to have the aid of his wife, Emily Roebling, who carried out his precise instructions and became, as McCullough observes, his devoted and vital "amanuensis." Although over the years Emily Roebling faithfully clipped out every article about the bridge and pasted the clippings in a scrapbook, the Roeblings never allowed a single journalist to enter their home for an interview, and because of their discretion, the only recorded bursts of feeling between them are hidden among many pages of technical information in the notebooks that Mrs. Roebling kept for her husband. We'll never understand the inner machinations of their partnership—how she managed her husband's frustrations (not to mention her own)—but it does seem that Washington and Emily Roebling eschewed nineteenth-century norms and were partners in the truest sense.

She was the first person to ride across the bridge in a carriage on May 24, 1883. As the horses trotted along on that fine spring morning, she held a rooster as a sign of victory. While gentle breezes blew and seagulls coasted overhead, Washington Roebling watched the ceremony unfold from his window in the Heights. It had been his request that his wife be the first to make the journey. Among his many names for her was "My own particular darling."

I call my grandmother's seventy-one-year-old niece. She remembers my great-grandmother as a refined woman, a snob who was never seen without makeup or a corset, and who (I assume she extrapolated) hated sex.

And the proposal? I ask. I try to steer the conversation, though lively, back to the story.

You know all this Fiddler on the Roof *crap? Well, she had no fondness for where she came from. She left her village when she was sixteen, speaking only Yiddish. She had never seen electricity or a train, but she was pretty and she knew it and she was afraid that she was going to be married off to some old slob, plucking chickens the rest of her life. This was a town where when they heard a noise, everyone looked up because it meant that a stagecoach was coming through. That was the big event of the day—you get the picture? No, she had no fondness for Eastern Europe, no nostalgia.*

*She came with her older sister and looked after her nieces
in exchange for her passage to America. She worked in a factory out in the sticks, but this was a girl who did not come to
America to marry some factory worker. She had red cheeks
and an hourglass figure, and she also had a relation or two in
New York.*

So the bridge, I say, *Brooklyn.* I'm not exactly sure what
I'm looking for, but if I stopped for a moment, I might realize that it's more than any one person can offer. Even
though my mother grew up seeing her grandmother regularly, she has startlingly little to say about her. From what
I've heard, I gather that my great-grandparents' marriage
was hardly the love story of the century. My grandmother
used to say her two sisters basically raised her, and when I
asked her why, she answered as if she had rarely considered the reasons. *My mother was tired,* was what she said.
My great-grandmother apparently spent an inordinate
amount of time in her room. She also lived to be nearly one
hundred years old.

I suppose I want to believe that she had some lovely
memories to consider during those quiet hours. I suppose—
I know it is childish—I want to discover that my great-
grandparents were crazy for each other, if only for that
instant when they were strangers on a bridge.

ON a crisp October evening at the end of the twentieth
century, my boyfriend, a born-and-bred Brooklynite (whose

forbears, while mine were plucking chickens in greater Lithuania and Warsaw, were, among other things, preaching the gospel in pockets of the south and creating the world's largest mule farm in Lathrop, Missouri), suggested we take a walk on the Brooklyn Bridge. He had crossed the bridge countless times—as a teenager on a bicycle (it was eventually stolen during one of those rides), and, later, in the back of a cab returning home from late nights in Manhattan. He had also, until recently, depicted its towers and cables in oil on canvas, oil on panel, study after study until he could hardly stand to look at it and took to painting the city from up above, the bridge no longer a subject but subsumed into fields of color. I loved to see his paintings on arbitrary Sundays, when we'd take long walks to his studio (first in DUMBO and then in Red Hook) and it was these paintings, as much as the walking, that helped me to focus on the neighborhoods, to appreciate, despite my horrendous sense of direction, how they related to one another. And so we took a walk in early October, and it was there on the Brooklyn Bridge that our own engagement story unfolded.

Of course memory doesn't focus, the way a story should, on a beginning, middle, and end. Memory is a flash of cobalt light and water, chilly air, and the feel of the coat I was wearing; it was wool, a robin's egg blue, with a '60s flair and slightly too-short sleeves. But that's not exactly it. I remember that as we were walking, my heart began speeding up and I thought—is he going to ask me to marry him right now? But as he was saying all kinds of romantic senti-ments, the specifics of which I have sadly forgotten, I remember thinking—no. No, this is a normal evening, this is just us; this is what we are like together. And then I' thought: *remember this*. I didn't want to forget that such a moment did not have to be the prelude to anything mo-mentous. Although, as it turned out, it was.

He didn't kneel, we were eye to eye. He asked, and I answered. I was sure. We were what they would have called in my great-grandmother's time a love match.

My boyfriend was familiar with the story of my great-grandparents' betrothal. I had told him with the same romantic zeal that now propelled me to find out more about their story. I am romantic but I am suspicious, and I had always liked to imagine what may or may not have hap-pened that night—theirs—on the Brooklyn Bridge. Was he taken with her beauty? Angry at being rejected by another girl? Was she so frightened of this new country that she would have married anyone?

OF course mine is hardly the only family whose mythology is tethered to the bridge. From an informal search, stories abound: it was the sight of Nate's proposal to Caroline just six months after their first date; Billy proposed to Annie at sunset; Sean asked Kelly in the middle of the night; and, after 9/11, when two volunteers for the Red Cross met and fell in love, the bridge became the site of their engagement too. How many couples have shared this magnificent one-half mile, which exists neither here nor there, while making such an important decision?

Even the language used to describe the bridge has had a consistently romantic bent. In an 1889 *Brooklyn Eagle* article detailing the reasons why Brooklyn should not be annexed to "New York": "The Brooklyn Bridge has so far helped Brooklyn that our sister city is now sparking us, hoping to be wedded to us, but she must first cleanse herself and put on her best before we will consider her suit."

In 1902, on the darker and more peculiar side of love, according to the *Brooklyn Eagle*, Frank C. Cody was "a colored man who jumped the bridge" because he had "deep pity for himself." "He loves his white wife," the reporter wrote, "who has deserted him twenty-eight times. . . . She said to him: 'Now, Frank, you say you love me. Why don't you show it. Why don't you go off the bridge if you love me . . .'" When, after surviving, he was charged with suicide, Cody cried to the magistrate in a Butler Street court of law, "Suicide? No, never! Never!" He explained that he was "entitled to a wreath of laurel rather than a pair of handcuffs," and, as was the fashion with those who jumped and lived to tell about it, "he made a bee line for a dime museum," where he could rely on an eager audience willing to pay for his curious tale.

Amid fame-seekers, suicides and thwarted suicides, and a handful of UFO sightings and alien abductions, I keep expecting to find, in the archives of the *Brooklyn Eagle*, a proposal story whose details match my great-grandparents'. I know this is ludicrous. I know that something so private and historically insignificant as an engagement between two unknowns would never have been recorded. I also know that it's precisely the ephemeral nature of such stories, their delicate threads handed down through generations like the silk purse I have from my grandmother, that draws us in. It's the not-knowing that makes us want to know.

WHEN Derek proposed, we had recently moved in together in Carroll Gardens. I had moved from the West Village of Manhattan, where I had never felt more at home. I liked Brooklyn, but couldn't imagine that living there wouldn't be more than a temporary experiment, an experience to share before moving back. Derek, though he never waxed rhapsodic about the borough (he never waxes rhapsodic, period), loved living in Brooklyn with the kind of love that is so long practiced, so intimate, that at first glance it can seem almost casual. It took me a while to understand why he seemed uncharacteristically confused when I fantasized about moving elsewhere. But ultimately, as the months passed, those fantasies faded because, as I began to release what I came to think of as an extra breath (the one I hadn't been aware of holding), as I emerged from the subway each day at dusk, I fell into my own love affair with the place, and once it took hold of me, I realized, almost with resignation, that it was already my home.

* * *

IT *was a Sunday afternoon*, my grandmother's niece tells me.

Not a dinner party?

No.

Because I always heard it was a party.

No. A Sunday afternoon.

Well, that sounds nice, I say, thinking of our Sundays— my boyfriend's and mine—walking, looking at paintings.

She visited some relations. That's how they met on the Lower East Side.

They didn't meet in Brooklyn?

No, no. Lower East Side. He'd come over when he was thirteen and did eight grades in one year. No dummy. His parents wanted him to marry a rabbi's daughter, something special, you know.

They weren't happy with his decision?

His sisters kept hanging around her because they thought she was wearing rouge and that if they stayed put long enough it would wash off.

But what happened that day? The day that he proposed?

I guess he took one look at her red cheeks and knockout figure and asked her to take a walk. He showed her his bank book.

His bank book?

I guess he wanted to prove he had savings.

It's hard not to wince. *But it was the Brooklyn Bridge? I*

realize, at this point, that I am starting to sound kind of desperate.

When she says, *No, no, it was the Williamsburg Bridge,* I'm surprised to find that I feel almost giddy. *Are you laughing?* my grandmother's niece asks.

I can't help it.

Why?

Because there is nothing left of my story, the story I have always known, and as much as it leaves me feeling empty, I also feel momentarily unburdened by what happened and what didn't. Because even as I try to glean some kind of truth about my great-grandparents, the story in itself is a bridge that exists outside of fact and memory, one that binds one generation to another until all we have is Manhattan on one side, Brooklyn on the other, and the darkness of the river below. Because these two people existed and no matter how long they'd known one another or where they were from, they must have stared at the city and their joined future, both of which must have loomed rather large. Because it was *their* moment—these two immigrants trying to impress one another, these two nice-looking kids, Ann and Albert—and no one (not even me!) really needs to know how it felt to be them right then. Because, for me, stories are serious business, and maybe I should lighten up.

I don't tell her this. I say thank you. I tell her, truthfully, that—after a lifetime of not knowing her—I'd love to see her soon. But as I hang up the telephone, as I look out my window at the spindly branches and sparrows and ancient clotheslines swinging through the Carroll Gardens sky, I'm no longer smiling. I wonder what will happen to our story—our October evening, our proposal, our engagement, our desires and fears, our private names, our petty arguments, our very good meals—our Brooklyn story, Derek's and mine. The story that—no matter how detailed or loving our descriptions—we will have to entrust, like a delicate heirloom, to our children.

A WINDSTORM IN DOWNTOWN BROOKLYN
Robert Sullivan

Most people like to look at mountain rivers, and bear them in mind; but few care to look at the winds, though far more beautiful and sublime, and though they become at times as visible as flowing water.

—JOHN MUIR, *A Wind Storm in the Sierras*

WHEN I GO out to look at the wind, I go to downtown Brooklyn. A lot of people living in New York City don't even know that there is a downtown Brooklyn, much less that it is an excellent place to watch the wind. That's because New York's celebrity downtowns are Wall Street and Times Square and maybe even Herald Square. In Brooklyn, downtownness is, generally speaking, dispersed, spread throughout various neighborhoods, and downtown Brooklyn, possibly as a result, is, on first glance, less spectacular-seeming, more workaday, more middle urban America. In the morning in downtown Brooklyn, into the streets and the triangle of green-but-mostly-cement park around the old classically columned Borough Hall, commuters rise up out of the subways and gently collide, "excuse me"-ing or sleepily silent, and they immediately come face-to-face with the wind. Even on nearly windless days, it is windy in downtown Brooklyn.

Naturally, when the wind blows, it blows everything and everybody, which makes wind watching a little like watching trout in a stream, a diversion unto itself. There are the small-time attorneys whose legal forms break free suddenly in the wind. Short and tall, in suits and ties that have done significant time, they buy their legal forms and Post-its and large file folders from the Hasidic computer ink-cartridge experts at Court Street Office Supplies; the lawyers hold their hands palm up and look into the glazed eyes of their clients while saying, "You could get seven years for a felony like that."

There are Arab-Americans on their way to Atlantic Avenue, the border of downtown Brooklyn, where there are Arabic CD stores, Syrian bakeries, Yemeni cafés, and Middle Eastern food emporiums filled with huge bins that are, in turn, filled with earth-colored grains and puckered dried fruits and glistening olives. Djellabas flapping in the wind, two men leave a Yemeni café, holding the tiny cups of tea like bowsprits before them. They cross Atlantic Avenue, which is a hill where it intersects with Court Street, looking west toward New York harbor, New Jersey, and the rest of America.

There are private-school parents from the three private schools within four blocks of each other in downtown

Brooklyn, the parents who drive cars designed for auto-bahns and ranch work and anxiously circle the crowded blocks in mini air-controlled climates. They drop their children into the wind; tiny unzipped down vests and jackets blow back but just short of off.

There are Caribbean-American Brooklynites who work at places like the Metropolitan Transit Authority or in the state, county, and federal courts. There are Caribbean-American Brooklynites who also drive or arrive via nearly every subway line from neighborhoods like Flatbush and Crown Heights and Bedford-Stuyvesant to push strollers carrying children who bear no familial resemblance to them. There is a woman from Trinidad, for example, who, one windy day, talked to me about the wind, the little boy she was minding walking just ahead. She compared a cold winter blast in downtown Brooklyn to a warm summer wind in her native country. She said she never, ever wore a sweater as a child, and then, while talking, suddenly recognized a fellow Trinidadian by the tune that he was whistling—and so, wind talk over.

And then there are the discount shoppers of downtown Brooklyn, the act of discount shopping being an act that is culturally unifying in itself, a human denominator. Downtown Brooklyn is the capital of discount shopping in New York. The great Fulton Mall stretches from Borough Hall to Flatbush Avenue, ending at Albee Square, an about-to-be-redeveloped square named for Edward Albee II, a one time ticket taker for P. T. Barnum, a vaudeville promoter

himself, as well as the adoptive grandfather of Edward
Albee, the playwright and author of *The American Dream*.
Fulton Mall is a stretch of old Brooklyn department stores
abandoned in the seventies and recolonized in the eighties
and nineties by discount electronics stores, discount shoe
stores, discount sneaker stores, discount hat stores, stores
that sell discounted goods at a discount. There are podia-
trists and dental clinics (WE SPECIALIZE IN COWARDS) and
places that sell inexpensive jewelry in the shape of fists,
fingers, and Jesus Christ. On Fulton Street in some places,
rents are higher than on Madison Avenue; Fulton Street is
the third-highest dollar-volume retail district in New York
City, with a hundred thousand shoppers a day, putting it, in
terms of human activity, on a par with Fifth Avenue, or, by
association, the Champs-Élysées. Studies show, however,
that the residents of the gentrified neighborhoods that sur-
round downtown Brooklyn rarely go to downtown Brooklyn. Thus, the city and developers deem it "underutilized."

But the wind blows no matter what the developers say,
ruffling hundreds of book covers at stands that sell books
and tapes and CDs that aren't seen in the non–Fulton
Street bookstores—like a homemade recording of Martin
Luther King's last speech, delivered to black sanitation
workers in Memphis, who were on strike for not getting
paid for days off due to inclement weather, even though
white workers did. See the raging wind hurtle fast-food
trash from McDonald's or the shreds of the Dunkin'
Donuts banner advertising fresh-baked chocolate-chip

cookies. But see too the winds introduce a blue bag from an upscale food market on Montague Street in Brooklyn Heights. Like the leaf of an invasive plant, the blue bag enters the stream of wind trash quietly, mingles with the other trash, gets caught under the wheel of a bus, then swept away by street-cleaning crews who act as if the windstorm weren't perpetual, as if their job weren't a lot like Sisyphus's job except without the downhill part.

Borough Hall is the capitol of Brooklyn and the capital of its downtown. The winds are visited by just-married couples buying flowers upon leaving the Kings County Municipal Building, by contractors and their workers looking for permits, by people who just paid their parking tickets. When an administrative judge who has just declared you guilty of double-parking on a street-cleaning day leaves the municipal building and enters the winds, he is greeted by tables and stands all around Borough Hall whose hand-made signs—marked "Handbags $10" or "$1 Silk Ties" or "Any Item: $5" or "Watches 2 for $5" or "Great Deal!" or "'Give-away' Prices"—vibrate like weather vanes on top of country barns as a vendor shouts over the current: "Come on, people! Take a look! Treat yourself *heeere!*"

Court Street runs through downtown Brooklyn like a spine, and on a clear day, you can almost see the wind racing up Court Street from the Brooklyn Bridge, pushing back strollers, recombing attorneys' hair—the tinglingly glorious wind that fingers a double-breasted suit on an outdoor sale rack and grabs it and attempts to run off with it toward the Brooklyn House of Detention. The apple farmer from Wiklow Orchards in Highland, New York, who drives cider and apples down to the farm stand in front of the stairs at Borough Hall three times a week, moves his wares from one side of his truck to the other, but then finally gives up, his bundled Scandinavian worker smiling and shivering in a big coat as the farmer packs to leave. A baker from the Hudson Valley loses a tray of organic Danish to the wind.

When it rains, the wind is ruthless; a trip from an office building down into the subway is a made-for-the-Weather-Channel arctic adventure or, in the summer, an expedition through a tropical storm. Umbrellas are useless in downtown Brooklyn, though umbrella owners never give up hope. One March afternoon, the rain started late, around four. At rush hour, when the commuters poured into the streets, the wind destroyed the smaller umbrellas at the very moment they were opened; in one hand-driven movement, the umbrellas went from working umbrellas to inside-out umbrellas, stripped of their black skirts. Larger umbrellas fought the wind valiantly for a few seconds, battling for a half a block or so before being closed or also destroyed. That night, at dusk, after the storm had stopped, Court Street had that just-squeegeed feel of a New York City street post-rain, a grimy cleanliness. And in the four-block stretch lay the workings of ninety-one umbrellas. (There may have been more—I didn't get to the bottom of a few of the more overstuffed garbage recep-

tacles filled with rain-soaked trash.) The broken chrome
workings reminded me of a beach on the Baja peninsula
that I once visited, a place where shipwrecks decorate the
cove like skeletal remains.

AS far as I'm concerned, the very best place to watch the
wind in downtown Brooklyn is near the corner of Montague and Court streets, an intersection not just of two
streets but of people, cars, buses, traffic cop cars (which
jam up the cars they are trying to ticket), and the winds.
The winds here are a result of the topography of the intersection, which sits on a hill that looks down into two man-
made, wind-tunneling valleys. To the northwest is the
narrow valley of brownstones and stately old apartment
buildings of Brooklyn Heights, a ferry ride in the nineteenth century from lower Manhattan, a first suburb, each
cross street allowing a glimpse of New York Harbor's white-
capped blue water. To the northeast is a great plain, a flat-
land manufactured not by erosion or glacial forces or
ancient sediments but by an old plan for urban renewal. In
the New York of the 1950s and '60s, big was better than
small; streamlined was better than nooks and crannies.
Thus, a series of what were called superblocks cleared out
the crowded streets of the *old* downtown Brooklyn, the
Brooklyn of Walt Whitman, and replaced them with a plot
of land that was supposed to be Brooklyn's Piazza San
Marco but ended up a lot lonelier and emptier and quite

frequently more rat-plagued: the Brooklyn of *The French Connection*. From the point of view of wind-watching, Cadman Plaza is a grand steppe, bounded by tall federal and state courts and giant housing projects, a place where the wind collects, gains speed, and gathers power before blowing east and blasting into the Rocky Mountains of businesses and municipal buildings all around Borough Hall. It is there, at the point where the two rivers of wind meet—precisely at the intersection of Court and Montague—that an invisible whirlpool of wind exists, a vortex made visible in the swirl of stray trash.

This vortex is not one of those tiny tornadoes of fallen leaves that scuttle trash on a lonely side street—the kind that pop up all over New York City, suddenly, silently, momentarily, like haiku. This vortex fills the air above it with sheets of newspapers and inflated plastic shopping bags that swim through it like manta rays and Portuguese men-of-war. When the wind is blowing, the intersection around and above Borough Hall looks like it's following a clothing label's instructions, "Tumble dry only." But there is a delicateness to the vortex also: see the gull-like circling of the small, square tissue papers used to place pastries into a customer's bag. At night, under the street lamp, flocks of newspapers separate and dance in daring, flowing rhythms reminiscent of Martha Graham.

A plastic bag's flight path through the vortex is as predictable as a 747's turn over the Jamaica Bay Wildlife Refuge before landing at JFK. The path goes like this: A bag blows northeast up Court Street. It begins to circle in the street, teasingly. First it is low, and then, by the start of the second lap, it is a few feet off the ground. The circle grows. The bag rises—one story and then in the next lap two stories, and then it is suddenly up six stories, at which point it is caught in a higher, stronger wind than the wind of the downtown Brooklyn vortex. It is the vortex at large, the vortex of the heavens.

The vortex appears and disappears, like the little darting whirlpool in the bottom of a draining bathtub. On one bright, clear windy day a few years ago, I watched a garbage truck collect demolition debris from an office building that stands on the corner of Court and Montague, the Court-Montague Building. When I first moved to Brooklyn, in the eighties (and when my uncle worked there, in the fifties), the Court-Montague Building was the second-tallest building in Brooklyn, a steep wedding-cake structure, and it had yet to grow its Mohawk of cell phone antennae. On that winter day, as laborers brought out container after container of former walls of the Court-Montague Building, as they brought out chunks of conference tables and beat-up file cabinets and clouds of dust, the hydraulics of the truck crushed everything, roaring and moaning. All through its labor, it hacked up black diesel smoke, which, instead of dispersing in a gentle breeze, made a sharp downward turn and collected and swirled in the vortex, like black ink in a drain. The path of soot and dust was so neat and smooth—a circle of black wind in an otherwise blue-sky morning—that I felt as if I were watching a science experiment. When morning commuters came upon the little black twister, they held down their heads and sprinted. It made me want to figure out a way to enter the vortex, which I eventually did.

IN the city, the wind is like a giant nudge, a full-body wink, an in-your-face and in-your-hair reminder that you live outdoors, that steam and electricity and water from faraway reservoirs and sewage aren't the only things that course through the city every day. Residents of other New York boroughs talk about their windiest spots—Eighty-sixth Street on the East Side; the elevated subway stop at Queensboro Plaza; East Tenth Street in Greenwich Village, where Broadway suddenly veers left. But the vortex of downtown Brooklyn reminds me that it's all the same, that the wind whips through the fields of New York just as it does, for instance, the red cliffs that frame the western edge of Boulder, Colorado.

In my own attempts to analyze the vortex, I have purchased various handheld wind-measurement devices over the years. The first was a cheap plastic model—not the kind of thing you would want for artillery work but it did the job. More recently, I acquired an electronic device designed to be used in golf, a sport I don't play. (I bought it at a discount electronics store in downtown Brooklyn.) I carry it with me on windy days. A typical reading near the vortex might be in the 9- to 15-mile-an-hour range. Readings at the main intersection can go as high as 25 miles an hour, especially in February and March.

Once, at the vortex corner, I took a few steps down Montague Street to read the wind coming in from the Northwest. It was a little over 20 miles an hour with gusts into the 40s, an excellent reading. I went out in the intersection but the wind device just blew all around out there, and I couldn't get anything. Downtown Brooklyn was charged with wind, and the place all seemed to be humming like a giant aeolian harp.

On a windy day the following February, I finally realized that the way to measure the vortex was to not measure it. It was a Saturday—clear sky, cool temperatures—and the car traffic was light and the schools of discount shoppers were small. A large circle of morning trash had appeared in the middle of Court Street: coffee lids, *Post* and *Daily News* pages, a few cellophane cigarette wrappers, and a dead, rat-like thing that I eventually realized was a toupee. When the traffic lights allowed, I stepped excitedly out into the street. The wind was raging again—the vortex sandblasting me with dust. Slowly and cautiously avoiding the oncoming traffic, I stepped farther through the trash ring and into the center of the circle, maybe ten feet in circumference. I can report that in the very center of the vortex there was absolutely no wind. The trash circled around me as if I were Mickey Mouse in *Fantasia*, and I like to think I felt a perfect windless calm.

* * *

WHAT does wind-watching matter? I certainly can't say.
The Hebrew word for wind is also the Hebrew word for
spirit, *ruah*, and when I look at the wind I look at something immeasurable, spiritlike, a climactic feature of a soul
or souls. Try as I may, I still can't predict the wind in downtown Brooklyn, nor can I even imagine how the wind blew
when Walt Whitman stepped out on the corner of Cran-
berry Street that is no longer there, or how it will feel when
downtown Brooklyn is redeveloped, or "utilized." I can feel
it though. Especially I can feel the vortex, which draws me,
calls to me. When it is windy elsewhere in New York or
the world and I am far from the vortex, I think of it, imagine the swirl. Often I walk my daughter, who is eleven,
through the vortex on her way back and forth to school,
even though it's a little out of our way—after years of
forced wind-watching, her older brother walks alone now,
noticing, I hope, the wind on his own. On Saturday mornings, if we go to the farmer's market, we buy doughnuts
and cider and sit on the benches in Columbus Park at the
steps of Borough Hall, and wait and see what the wind will
blow up. We face the Court-Montague Building and a
London plane tree whose branches are notable among
Brooklyn trees for their lack of plastic shopping bags. The
wind rips the bags away.

Six years ago, I was with my son, who was ten at the time,
and we were on our way to his school when I saw an entire
stack of newspapers go up into the air, a trashy celebration!
We were on Court Street, just about to the corner of Mon-

tague, when we passed a newsstand. The man selling the papers was doing a pretty good job holding down copies of the *Times* and the *Post* considering he had the not-so-good idea of setting up a newsstand inside the vortex, but he was having trouble with the *Daily News*, which eventually escaped, almost the whole stack, and was then whipped quickly and frantically into the vortex. In a second, the corner of Court and Montague had headlines all over it, the pages doing flip-flops, and then floating out into the street. In another second the sheets of paper began flying up, up, up. My son and I stepped back from the building and waited and watched as, at last, one sheet slowly climbed all forty-two stories of the Court-Montague Building. (A couple of days later, the newsstand relocated two blocks away.)

Believe me, the vortex is not just in my imagination. I have seen other people seeing the vortex, and I know a historian who refers to the vortex as the gartex, on account of all the garbage. Indeed, over the years, my family and I have shared many vortex moments with people who have likewise shared theirs. A windstorm in downtown Brooklyn is a public thing, a well-known phenomenon. I still recall the day my then five-year-old daughter alerted me to a silver helium-filled Mylar balloon that had been caught in the widening gyre and, as we watched, lifted off into the New York City heavens. It was her very first vortex sighting. We watched the balloon rise up and over the Court-Montague Building and then at last escape into the open blue sky over Borough Hall and downtown Brooklyn at large, a rare silvery bird rising up on its way.

DOWN THE MANHOLE
Elizabeth Gaffney

WHEN I WAS a girl, we sometimes went out on rubbing expeditions. Our target: manhole covers. My mother, a graphic designer and artist and a gifted impresario of outings, orchestrated these events, while my father, an artist and college art professor, provided the materials: huge pads of rice paper and various large charcoal sticks and Conté crayons that he pilfered from a vast store of supplies ordered for the benefit of his undergraduates. Around this same time, my father was getting involved in a teachers' union and picketing his own campus in a T-shirt stenciled with a red fist and the word *strike*. He was smoking hashish and painting beautiful, terrifying pictures. He was reading Marvel comics and talking about peace in Southeast Asia. He had long hair and little round glasses and was a member of a co-op gallery in SoHo, when SoHo was for art, not shopping. He was too young and maybe not quite cool enough to be a beatnik, too old by a shade to be a hippie. I suppose it's possible my father actually bought the art supplies, or maybe my mother did, but I like to think that he liberated them from the supply closet as compensation in lieu of fair wages.

And then we went out and made imprints of manhole covers all across downtown Brooklyn. Some had writing that identified their function, some just cryptic initials, some beautiful floral or rhythmic graphic elements whose practical purpose was, I presume, to provide pedestrian traction and perhaps even advertising. I have no idea anymore how many such outings took place. There may have been just a few, but their message was fixed in my mind like a Kosmocrete logo in cast iron: go out and look at the world. Really see it—especially things otherwise likely to go unnoticed. It was about awareness, it was about engagement, it was about making art out of everyday life. The rubbings we made were prominently posted by my mother on the floor-to-ceiling corkboard in her studio, along with an ever-morphing collage of her own designs, drawings, and photographs as well as clippings of interesting typography or graphic design.

These were perfect outings for the child I was: we were mucking around in the dirt, on the street. We were being a bit subversive, it seemed to me, since one member of our expedition often had to stop or redirect traffic. We were making pictures, and miraculously we were doing it entirely without creative anxiety, thanks to the fact that the images were borrowed from the pavement and from the past. Our contribution consisted of noticing them, framing them on our page, and deciding how hard to press.

My parents, as artists, were eager to have their children out discovering beauty in the pedestrian, complexity in the mundane, and they understood child psychology pretty well. Looking for these things underfoot, where few expected to find anything of value, was just the right kind of fun and worked better than yet another trip to the MoMA. We didn't have to behave. We were allowed, nay required, to touch. My parents believed that embedding beautiful designs in the asphalt and the sidewalks was a quin-tessentially democratic, political act. When we went out, we considered not just manhole covers but fire hydrants, alarm boxes, street and traffic lights, signage. They were interested in urban renewal and preservation, and so the ideas of street furniture and the livability of the street were important to them. We rated what we saw, and talked about why we did or didn't like it. To me, the very idea of street furniture was thrilling—it conjured images of nestling in the cushions of imaginary street-corner sofas and jumping on nonexistent double beds. My mother in particular was also a history buff, and so the connection of the manhole covers to Brooklyn's past was important. Most of them were old; we tried to figure out exactly how old from the names on them and the wear they had undergone. Some were rubbed so smooth there was nothing to make a rubbing of, and my mind boggled to think of the forces that could scrape such heavy metal down to nothing. When my mother explained that the metal wheels of horse-drawn vehicles wore the street down harder than modern rubber

tires filled with air, I was catapulted into a new under-
standing of a previous era. The past had never seemed very
believable to me, until then. People might have gone
around riding horses and wearing bonnets somewhere out
West, say where *Little House on the Prairie* had transpired,
but not on the streets I inhabited. But thanks to manhole
covers and several stretches of street still paved with Belgian blocks, not asphalt—also pointed out by my mother—
I could suddenly fathom that Brooklyn had been something
different once too. History had happened here.

One of the most crucial questions manhole covers
raised for me was below the surface. I wanted to go down
under them, to find out where they led. It was a little
beyond the purview of our outings, however, and I never
got further than a few chats with the guys from ConEd
or BUG, the local gas company. The workmen generally
indulged a young girl's interest and tolerated a glance down
their holes while repair work was going on, but no one ever
allowed me to venture down there. To reward our curiosity,
my brother and I were given books by our parents about
the world beneath the city, some about New York in particular and others that covered various types of infrastructure
in some depth, including some fairly specific illustrations
of how sewage was processed (in those days, not nearly
enough). But I was never sated. I never lost the yearning to
see for myself what went on beneath the street, and especially my street.

Some years ago, when I began writing a novel set in

New York in the nineteenth century, I found myself unex-
pectedly setting much of it in the sewers. Of course, not all
manholes lead to the sewers: there's gas, electric, water,
and nowadays even cable down there as well, but water
and sewers were first. I put water aside—too well documented already. Furthermore, I had happened onto a
couple of vivid accounts of how bad the city smelled back
then, and I decided to follow my nose. The sewers, I found
out, were not designed very intelligently, at first. In fact,
they were hardly designed at all. It so happened that I was
reading mostly about Manhattan's sewers. Manhattan
seemed better documented in general, and I just assumed
without thinking much about it that Manhattan and
Brooklyn would be in roughly the same boat, sewagewise.

I learned that aside from a few early efforts, such as the
one that gave Canal Street its name, most of the city's early
sewers were privately constructed, and there was no mas-
ter plan until well past mid-century. As a result, the system
was not, strictly speaking, a system. The need for sewers in
New York greatly increased after the Croton Reservoir
project brought upstate water to the entire grid of Manhattan in 1842. According to their means and their predilec-
tions, people brought the water from the mains to their
houses for kitchens and bathrooms. But there was no man-
date to put in sewer lines at the same time, nor did the city
introduce any means for treating the wastewater outflow.
Soon, the water table began to rise with very dirty water.
Some wealthy people had big sewers hooked up to their

homes and businesses, hoping to drain away effluvia swiftly and keep their environments clean, but if their neighbors didn't or couldn't do the same, it was to no effect. A clog downstream would impact everyone upstream, regardless of social standing. All manner of pipes and connections were deployed, with an utter lack of awareness of hydrodynamics, making clogs the norm, not the exception. The whole thing was a disaster. Many poor neighborhoods at the edges of the city encompassed low-lying marshes that were plagued with overflows. Fecal-oral-spread diseases such as typhoid and cholera were rampant.

And then, while perusing a dissertation on the construction of the New York sewers, I came upon a reference to the excellent sewer system of Brooklyn. I was reminded of a fact I'd known all along: Brooklyn and Manhattan were separate cities, then, and anything but similar. It turns out that while Manhattan was a cesspool, Brooklyn was not. I looked deeper into the Brooklyn sewers, and the further I went, the prouder I grew. Brooklyn's sewers were the gold standard of that era. The initial twenty square miles of sewerage was designed in 1857 by Civil War veteran Colonel Julius Walker Adams, who later wrote *Sewers and Drains for Populous Districts*, the nineteenth century's definitive textbook on the topic. He studied fluid dynamics; he studied the pros and cons of using water to carry waste through the system; he studied the toxicity of gasses that accumulated in sewers and how to vent them. He even tabulated the volume of excreta produced by cities of various populations, broken down into liquid and solid waste and by gender and age, and specified the size and shape of sewer pipes required to handle it. In Brooklyn he introduced visionary technologies: vitreous clay pipes that let the sewage (and the troublesome flotsam) slide along its route far better than other materials. He created a system that tapered toward its extremities and widened and flowed downhill toward the outlets to adequately manage the actual volumes flowing through the system at each location. This issue of needing the stuff to flow smoothly away may seem obvious, but it was new, then. No one had worried about bottlenecks overflowing or sludge coming out of suspension to form clogs where water meandered too slowly. The only flaw in Adams's design was that some of the outlets were below the tide line, which was a problem when storms sent large volumes of water through the conduits, only to find the outlets closed till ebb tide. Adams was born in Massachusetts, but he designed Brooklyn's sewers and remained in charge of them for many years. He was the borough's own underground genius, and he singlehandedly took the art of sewage management in America forward into the modern era.

The one disappointment for me, in finding out how great Brooklyn's sewers were, was that I wanted to set my novel in a clogged and fouled sewer system, a place where unfortunate troglodytes were compelled to haul the muck away in buckets, where methane explosions might rock the tunnels and putrid gasses threatened lives. It meant that I ended up focusing far more on Manhattan in my novel than I, as a loyal Brooklynite, otherwise would have. Brooklyn's sewers were just too good to be really interesting. I did come across some fascinating Brooklyn sewer disasters in my research—the borough expanded swiftly, doubling in size from 1860 to 1870, necessitating plenty of new construction. I could have written an entire novel about the following headline from the *New York Times*, in November of 1908 (and I still may): "BROOKLYN EXPLOSION ENGULFS A SCORE—Men, Women, and Children Go Down under Flood, Fire, and Earth in Gold Street Sewer. Victims buried under tons of debris fifty feet down, while many slide into death pit." The excavation for the thirteen-and-a-half-foot-diameter trunk sewer was about fifty feet deep and thirty feet wide. Either a collapse of the trench ruptured a gas main, or an independently occurring gas leak was ignited by a spark from the excavation work. It was never determined for sure. There was a list of names, ages, and home addresses of the victims, including a group of six- and seven-year-olds: Clarice Brady, Vincent Doherty, John O'Grady, and William Dalton, who lived in two adjacent buildings near the disaster. I can picture them out together, a little gang adventurously exploring the margins of the work site just before it blew, the same way I would have at their age. Sixty off-duty telephone operators were called in to contact some ten thousand customers of the local gas company, to urge them to turn off all gas cocks, lest further fires and poisoning ensue after service was restored. The Borough Inspector of Sewers was there when the disaster happened and died with the rest of his workers, a fact that suggests a promising plotline rife with political scandal and intrigue. Maybe I'll write it one day, but when I came across the incident, I was already committed to a story set at the time of the Brooklyn Bridge's construction, so I let the 1908 explosion go. I focused instead on the expansion of Manhattan's dysfunctional tunnels in the post–Civil War period. It was good fun, finding out which of Manhattan's streets had tunnels with a large enough bore to let a gangster crawl through them. Still, I wished there was some way to bring my sewer research home, to Brooklyn. Even after I'd finished my novel, I wanted to go down there.

I've tried to get down into the sewers on and off for years, but it's not so easy. I've seen documentaries and pretty much every piece of film footage ever shot under New York, but I still haven't seen my dark, damp Mecca with my own eyes. There was a time that the city offered a mini-training session on entering confined spaces and took curious professionals with half-decent excuses on tours. I came around too late for that. Even writers who've covered the topic for serious news outlets have had a hard time getting access since 9/11. For me, a mere novelist interested in history, legal entry has proven impossible so far. Instead, I've had to make do with Paris, where the highlight of a romantic getaway weekend for me and my husband a couple years back was a tour of the Musée des Égouts—an institution after my own heart, not just dedicated to but located in the sewers. All right, it wasn't exactly the highlight of my husband's itinerary, but he consented to go along. I marveled at the exhibits detailing the evolution of flow management and sludge decomposition through the centuries. I exclaimed at the fresh and unsewerlike whiff of the effluent rushing beneath our feet and gathering in fog banks in the cool tunnels. He groaned and registered his eagerness to go back aboveground and wash his hands as soon as possible, then go sit in a café.

Now we have a daughter of our own who has lately begun putting sentences together, telling stories, and scribbling with markers and crayons. Before I know it, it will be time for me to spearhead some fabulous and inspiring art expeditions. I look forward to teaching her all about the city she lives in and showing her that an urban childhood can be as much of an idyll as the clichéd suburban one. I'll enjoy making sure she's aware of the infrastructure that enables us all to live in such splendid density: the buildings, the roads, the trains, the tunnels. I'm still proud of Brooklyn's sewers for having been among the best in the world, once, but I'm sorry to say I won't be able to brag about our borough's sewers to my daughter. As with many old big cities, New York City's combined wastewater system is badly outmoded. The ideal system has one set of pipes for wastewater from toilets and drains, which gets treated, and a second one for storm runoff. The trouble with doing it the old way, as we do here, is that whenever it rains, even just a little, the volume flowing through the pipes overwhelms the treatment plants and raw sewage shoots into the harbor, causing health and environmental problems.

Maybe it's a parent's fear of pathogens that might harm her child, or just the fact that I've changed so many diapers in the past couple years, but I don't hear the Siren song of the sewer tunnels so acutely these days. I love Brooklyn's beauty more now, and generally choose parks and gardens and bridges over crime and guts. When I eventually take my own daughter out to the streets to make manhole cover rubbings, I expect I'll emphasize the design element, just as my parents did, rather than where the tunnels beneath lead. If Lucy should decide to follow her own nose down into the underworld, I'd be thrilled. She's a ballsy little girl, and I can imagine her going where I never did. Maybe she'll even bring me along. Until then, I'll be content to enjoy the city's grandest sewers the way they were designed to be used: from a healthy distance.

A TRUE STORY
Darin Strauss

THIS IS A story about what one chooses to believe.

My grandmother's father played for the Brooklyn Kings before the team found the name by which you know them: the Dodgers. He was their first baseman. That was the legend I grew up on, anyway.

It was the crack of the twentieth century. Manny Joseph, the only Jewish King, got razzed during away games. Catchers would mutter "kike" and worse when my great-grandfather stood to bat; fans yelled all the old insults.

A different Brooklyn yeshiva boy, Sandy Koufax, arguably the best lefty ever to pitch (or, *in*arguably if you're a Jew of a certain age, a certain intensity of allegiance), won with the Dodgers half a century later. A pious Jew with ears like handles on a loving-cup trophy—old-world ears; Franz Kafka ears—Sandy Koufax skipped out on a desperate World Series opener to worship in synagogue; the game had fallen on Yom Kippur, the Jewish Day of Atonement. This act of steep piety made him a hero—better yet, a *mensch*—in Hebrew school circles.

My great-grandfather held different priorities. On
another Yom Kippur—at the start of my great-grandfather's
career and the twentieth century—the Brooklyn Kings'
Jewish first baseman sneaked from temple to sit for a team
photo. I cherish a copy of that picture. Dapper in his straw
hat and intricate necktie, Manny Joseph is the only player
not wearing cleats, a Kings cap, or the old-fashioned leather
mitt that looked like a cartoon-swollen hand—the habili-
ments of Brooklyn baseball, circa 1900.

And if he's not exactly handsome among his scruffier
teammates, his black-and-white face is lighted by one of
those rakish half smiles so beneficial to a good boy's looks
when he's acting naughty, or thinks he is. Holidays he
never cared for, he didn't like his wife, but baseball was my
great-grandfather's delight.

Or so the story goes.

LIKE the D. H. Lawrence character, his daughter (my
grandmother) was beautiful and had been given all the
advantages, yet she had no luck. She married for love, and
the love blew away.

By the time I popped into the world, she was an alco-
holic, a hermit who wouldn't quit referring to my grandfather as her husband, though by then he'd already left her
for the woman who'd become his wife in every sense but
the legal one. She lived alone for the next three musty

decades in the big Long Island house that my grandfather had built for her and then abandoned her to.

I always dreaded going over to see my drunken grand-mother. She often got fantastically cruel; once, she told me that I hadn't been as smart as my dad was, or as good an athlete. I *was* an unathletic, wistful kid—thin as soup-kitchen consommé. With a hunter's precision my grand-mother targeted the little rifts in the sides of her relatives' confidence. (My father was a star high-school basket-ball player and eventually became the NCAA's Mason-Dixon hurdling champion in 1960; I never even *watched* sports.)

When I was a teenager my grandmother sobered up (broken hip; the cold turkey of a hospital stay). After that, she had a much nicer vibe. Her new gentleness clipped the wings of my animosity. She lived four towns over from me, a seven-mile bike ride. I'd go over and we'd talk a lot, some-times about her father's baseball career. That's probably what got me into the game; now, I watch the Yankees prob-ably a hundred times a year.

She was a grand lady, even in her hermit years. She had fine china, a maid she couldn't afford, and a large house in constant disrepair. She was vain of her move from a Flat-bush apartment to that big Long Island house. She died in 2000, and one of the last things she said to me was: "Why would you move back to Brooklyn, when all we wanted to do growing up was get out of there?" But that struck me as a pose, a shielding posture she'd put on like a catcher's mask. Brooklyn, her past—as mythic to her as Greece and Rome—was all she had. She talked about it with the glassy face of someone watching a favorite movie. The stickball games that neighborhood boys played, the schoolgirls watching them and giggling, their long skirts flapping as they ran from the immodest home-run hitters when they asked for kisses; Prospect Park, crowded and carefree, elated with sunlight; the Italian boys whistling as my young grandmother passed; the Jewish boys who averted their eyes, but not quickly enough. And, of course, the night pilgrimages into Manhattan, to see Sinatra, to see Benny Goodman. In the end, the past was her whole life: old scenes, dissolve cuts, fade-outs. She died talking about her husband—who, eighteen months earlier, had himself died in the arms of his live-in girlfriend of twenty-seven years, near his Manhattan apartment.

MY own dad knew his baseball-playing grandfather only when he was very young and the ex-player was very old. Bald, tired Manny Joseph would talk reluctantly about his sports years, his life before the insurance job, before my grandmother was born. He'd lean his hands on his kitchen table, his peanut head a little dropped. "It was great thing," he'd say, huffing to stand. "But it's over now, so . . ."

Besides the team photo of him, the only other image left of Manny Joseph shows a man stooped under his eighty-

odd years, with the body—five-four, slim hips, a big belly—
of a schoolgirl eight months into a mistake.

To find out more about his playing days, I schlepped last
year to the library at Cooperstown's Baseball Hall of Fame.
And this is where the story, like all family stories, gets complicated.

"There is no Manny Joseph here," said the impartial
librarian, her eyes creeping like snails over a fat book of
names listing anyone who has ever played professional
baseball in America. It was as impressively bound as you'd
imagine, this Saint Peter's roll of all who'd made their way
past the exalted gates and into the major leagues.

"And," this woman said, with a voice seemingly practiced at killing the already slain, "the Brooklyn Dodgers
came from a team called the Superbas, not the Kings."

I went home dejected, of course; doing research online,
I couldn't find the Brooklyn Kings anywhere, let alone
Manny Joseph. I decided not to tell my dad or his siblings.
Why ruin the one good memory we have of my grand-
mother's family?

And yet, in writing this piece, I figured I'd give it one
more shot. I found, online, a site called "Major League
Baseball Franchise Information." It reads that the Brooklyn Dodgers *were* called the Hanlon's Superbas from
1899–1910, but also that one of their "nicknames"—
whatever that means—was the Brooklyn Kings, in the
1880s. I don't think Manny Joseph would have been old
enough to play in the 1880s, but I don't know. Also, had I

asked about Emmanuel Joseph? I think so, but I can never be sure when it comes to my own spaciness. Also, I *do* have that photograph: the team with "Kings" inscribed on their chests, and the one young Jew with them, wearing a smile and his Yom Kippur best.

One thing I do know: he loved talking baseball. The last day of his last season, a Sabbath night, my great-grandfather Manny Joseph played his best game. He went five-for-five and squibbed out the game winner, a wounded little pop-up that barely dodged the shortstop's glove.

"Thanks God he didn't catch it," my great-grandfather said, for years afterward.

UNDERWOOD PARK: THE FIRST 12,000 YEARS

Susan Choi

ICE

BY THE TIME Dexter and I reach the park, in the earliest years of the twenty-first century, all the ice has melted. Silty water has streamed forth, making Flatbush and Coney Island, and joined up with the sea. Foreign rocks with no documentation have dropped out of the slush and settled here, far south of where they used to be. The ground on which we stand has accumulated enough soil and rubble and sand to be some of the highest in Brooklyn, and has even accumulated the name Brooklyn, and more specifically, the apt name Clinton Hill.

True, hills in Brooklyn are measured in tens and not hundreds of feet above sea level. But Clinton Hill's very subtlety lets it insinuate itself into our thoughts in the stealthiest ways. Dexter and I, on our way to the park, pause at the corner of Lafayette and Vanderbilt avenues, Dexter riding in the stroller before me: we look north up Vanderbilt, toward where the ice by degrees shrank away, and see

crenellated Manhattan, touched gold by the afternoon sun!
Perfectly framed by the avenue's trough is the Empire State
Building. Being Clinton Hillites we're accustomed to glori-
ous vistas; and we can feel the elevation in our legs if we
pay close attention. At least I can, pushing Dexter east up
Lafayette from the region of the Williamsburgh Savings
Bank Tower. There really is an incline; I'm not just out of
shape. I both see it and feel it once we've crossed Vanderbilt and gone another block east to the corner of Clinton:
the down-dipping line of the Lafayette rooftops and road.
Glad acceleration: Dexter and I are headed downhill again.
Clinton Hill isn't quite Appalachia, but in the context of a
seemingly sea-level city, any small topographical features
are pretty exciting.

At last Underwood Park has come up on the left. It's our
hillside oasis, though again we must be keen to take note
of the hill. The city clearly attempted to level the playground, but it still runs very slightly downhill from west to
east. Dexter and I have learned not to play "baseball" on
the west side of the play structure, because the fat plastic
"baseball" always winds up beneath the play structure's
ramps. North-south, the park is broken in two separate
tiers, the northern a short flight of steps higher up than the
southern. The upper tier at first glance also looks to be
level, but walk, again, toward the eastern side's gate: a sudden downslope that inspires recent converts from crawling
to walking to break into a short, thrilling run.

Twelve thousand years ago—plus or minus a millennium—the Ice Sheet, having scraped its way south from the pole, picking up all those strange northern rocks on the way; having gouged what it couldn't dislodge; having dislodged and absorbed anything not tied down; reached the southernmost point of its conquest, which turned out to be Brooklyn. Here, in Brooklyn, the great Ice Sheet stopped. Some elaborate mixture of circumstance halted the sheet's inexorable movement. Looking east, the frontier between Ice and Not Ice stretched the length of Long Island and bent north, toward the hook of Cape Cod. Looking west, the frontier crossed the harbor, had some part in the making of Sandy Hook, then struck out across Jersey. But not before shaping the borders of Brooklyn, and its inland contours: its flat Flatbush and its upraised Crown Heights. And its subtle Clinton Hill, upon whose gentle slopes sits the east-slanting Underwood Park.

When Dexter and I first become real park patrons—this is when he has first learned to walk—it's October, brisk and limpid, scent of snow on the wind, and so it's not impossible to imagine the great Ice Sheet rearing its head. Underwood Park, in the 1950s, was planted with oak trees, and in autumn the acorns rain down with such force that they bounce. The Clinton-Washington station of the G train lies under our feet, but so does the Ice-shaped terrain. Human beings can invent subway trains, and dig tunnels, and regrade the earth in two tiers that are supposed to be level. But they never can change everything. An Ice Sheet built the rise the park sits on; built the park, in a way.

Close your eyes and perhaps you can hear it: the pops and
cracks like the firing of cannon, as the stories-high sheet
begins melting and cleaving; the rush of meltwater honey-
combing its underside; the loud tumbling of strange northern rocks as at last they're released from the ice's great
body, to begin to rebuild their new home.

THE BLIND COUNTESS

"I am desperate because I find myself almost without black paper."

THE historical record shows little of importance pertaining
to the creation of Underwood Park for the next eleven
thousand, eight hundred years. Then, in 1808, comes the
invention of carbon paper.

Those few scholars on whom we rely for the story of the
Countess Carolina Fantoni da Fivizzono—namely Michael
Adler (*The Writing Machine*) but also Wilfred A. Beeching
(*Century of the Typewriter*)—are curiously tactful, or perhaps chivalrous, when it comes to the potent details of the
countess's influence. We know that she was young and
beautiful, and struck by blindness "in the flower of" that
youth and beauty (Adler). We can surmise that she was
also a woman of such passions as are not to be discouraged
by the absence of sight. She "carried on a copious correspondence," and *"felt a pressing need"* for something that
might enable her to continue to do so even once she lacked
sight (Beeching; lurid emphasis mine). It was a young man

named Pellegrino Turri of Castelnuovo whose unprece-
dented ingenuity enabled Countess Carolina "to corre-
spond with her friends (including him) *in private*" (Adler;
again; emphasis mine). How many times in the history of
love has the lover been forced—by personal incapacity, or
perhaps by external restraint—to speak the most intimate
language of passion, to the object of love, via *somebody
else*? I recall reading, with my heart in my throat and my
eyes blurred with tears, the anguished love letters of war-
wounded soldiers who'd been forced to dictate to an
embarrassed third party, most often a nurse. What an awkward triangle, when the unwanted, indispensable witness
is ushered into the furnace of love. Countess Carolina, I
imagine, wanted no such intrusion, though I also imagine
that, being a countess, her quotidian life was observed to
its smallest detail by a phalanx of servants. But some things
are too sacred even for servants to see. Signor Turri must
have agreed. His invention, an automatic writing machine
that used special "black paper" that he also devised, is generally credited as the first typewriter and the first carbon
paper, a combination that would go on to wreak massive
change on many millions of lives besides those of Pellegrino and Carolina ("*I am desperate,*" Carolina wrote to him
in November of 1808, "*because I find myself almost without
black paper*").

By the 1870s it was possible, in the United States, to
achieve wealth and success simply by specializing in carbon
paper, ribbons, and other typewriter accoutrements, which

were now being manufactured by a slew of firms, most notably Remington. But almost all typewriters of this period—the Caligraph, the Yost, the Sholes & Glidden, and the Remington, too—used a technology that had the type bars (those metal sticks with the letters on the end) striking the underside of the platen, or printing surface. This meant the typist, to see what had been typed, had to lift up the carriage to look. This sort of machine was called an "understroke" or "blind" writer—would that Countess Carolina (d. 1841) had lived to relish the irony! Efforts to perfect a "visible" machine—with which the typist could see what he or she typed while still typing—preoccupied the industry, but it was not until the mid 1890s that a German immigrant named Francis X. Wagner, working with his son, solved the "visibility problem" with a successful "forward stroke" model he first offered to Remington. Remington was enjoying success with their "invisible" model and didn't want to rock the boat, so Wagner offered his revolutionary design—which, according to Beeching, "has been incorporated in all successful standard and portable typewriters ever since"—to a typewriter-supplies manufacturer named John T. Underwood.

The so-called Underwood typewriter went on to become the most successful typewriter the world had yet seen, the paradigmatic typewriter, unseated in this regard only by the introduction of the IBM Selectric in 1961. Underwood himself went on to become an even wealthier man than he already was. (What about Francis X.? Alas, history—or

at least, the history that I've read—never says.) Underwood became a pillar of Brooklyn and a doer of good works
on a grand scale—he specialized in educating poor disadvantaged Koreans and poor disadvantaged Kentucky
Appalachians, two groups never before or since linked. But
before all this he married a Brooklyn socialite named
Grace Brainerd, and moved into her family's mansion,
which sat on a slight rise at 336 Washington Avenue, in
Clinton Hill, Brooklyn. The house was thereafter known as
the Underwood mansion.

Being a writer, I've always fetishized antique typewriters. Since college I've been lugging a few around, beetle-
like things with their shiny black carapaces and their
bristling type bars. I happen to have an old Underwood, in
need of a good bath of WD-40, but the last time I checked,
it still worked. When I was young it was the totem of my
writerly ambitions; now it reminds me of my naive, preten-
tious youth. When I first started to write seriously, I did a
lot of research on the Korea of my father's youth, about
which I wanted to write a novel, and discovered that the
Underwood family and their money were all mixed up in it,
busy converting hapless Koreans to Christianity wherever
they could. I remember looking at my Underwood typewriter and feeling confirmed, in some way: maybe I'd
chosen the right subject. Maybe I'd succeed, after all. Ten
years later, when I was pregnant with Dexter, I waddled
out of the ramshackle apartment my husband and I had
just bought, in such haste and hysteria that we hadn't even

managed to examine its immediate neighborhood; all we knew was that we could afford it. A week away from going into labor I staggered through the midsummer heat to the first oasis I came across, a paradise of towering oak trees, sparkling fountains, shaded benches, and joyous children. This was Underwood Park, just one block from the apartment where we were going to raise our son. We hadn't even known it was there.

DOWNHILL AND UP

CLINTON Hill is one of those Brooklyn neighborhood stories featuring dramatic decline, and dramatic revival, but as a partisan I find its story more dramatic—its terrain a lot steeper—than those of rivals like Brooklyn Heights or Park Slope. For one thing, there were multiple declines and revivals, and for another, the grandeur with which Clinton Hill started was pretty extreme. Even before the construction of the showpiece brick-and-limestone mansions that survive—the residences of the Bishop of Brooklyn and Pratt Institute's president, side by side on Clinton Avenue, for example—there had already waxed and waned a previous era of huge, fanciful villas of wood, built in the 1840s and '50s on deep, grassy lots on the wide, widely spaced avenues, which had been laid out as a pastoral suburb, to which Brooklyn Heights titans might retreat for a healthful respite. Back then the hill-ness of Clinton Hill, subtle as it always has been, was a principal selling point: the Hill elevated its lucky elite above supposed miasmas of dirt and disease.

Once Brooklyn was absorbed into greater New York, in 1898, downtown Brooklyn declined as a financial center and many of its titans relocated entirely to Manhattan. The villas—with their gardens, their fountains—were sold off and torn down. But there were still Brooklyn-based wealthy people, like John T. Underwood, and there was also the burgeoning middle class. "Country villas" gave way to elaborate mansions, and to equally lovely, if slightly more democratic, apartment buildings. Clinton Hill turned more urban, and a bit more diverse—if the mixture of really rich people and simply comfortable people can be considered diversity.

My own apartment building was built in 1890, on the site of a former single-family mansion, and was named "The Richelieu"—a funny clue to the class of aspirational people I imagine first lived in it. By the late 1970s, as far back as the collective memory of my current neighbors extends, the Richelieu had been bowed, if not broken. Her painted gold letters above the front door spelling THE RICHELIEU had almost worn away. They were soon gone completely. Several of her rambling, grand apartments—with their pocket doors and eleven foot ceilings, their transoms and their intricate plaster reliefs—stood empty. She'd been plundered for almost all her exquisite Victorian light fixtures. Her plaster had crumbled and her woodwork lay buried beneath drab coats of paint.

Clinton Hill overall had dramatically changed, like much

of Brooklyn in the course of the twentieth century, but only some of those changes were negative. On the plus side, in my opinion: rich whites left Clinton Hill and made room for a true range of people, of many classes and races. On the minus: with a decline in wealth came a predictable increase in crime and deterioration. But there's a plus to the minus side, too: benign neglect preserved much of the grandeur of the Hill, if in a compromised state. My Richelieu survived without becoming subdivided, without having her interior white-boxed; she's still a little bedraggled, battle-scarred, but you can tell what she was.

Just two blocks away, though, at 336 Washington Avenue, John T. Underwood's mansion succumbed. Interestingly, the death was self-inflicted, and though the motives were questionable, I think Clinton Hill gained, in the end.

John T. Underwood died in 1937, leaving his wife, Grace, and their only child, Gladys. Grace kept the mansion until the 1950s, at which point she made arrangements to have it demolished and to donate the site to the city for use as a park. I don't know whether, by then, her mansion's immediate neighbor, the Graham Home, had yet become what it would be by the late 1970s: a very nicely housed brothel. Even so, I imagine that Grace had a sense of the changes in store. The Parks Department's Deputy Chief of Operations for Brooklyn is a neighbor of mine named Tom Ching. Tom remembers a Parks historian telling him, of the Underwood women, that they were (in Tom's words) "pretty insular people. They were devastated by the changes in the neighborhood. And they seemed to feel that the house was *their* house, and should never be anything else." Even before talking to Tom Ching I'd heard, in that ambient way that you hear things, that Grace Underwood had had her house torn down rather than let it suffer the indignities of the neighborhood's changes. Whether fairly or not, I've always caught a whiff of stark racism off of this rumor. Of course there's no telling. Does it actually matter? Only if you want to underscore the pleasant irony of how things turned out: Underwood Park stuffed with kids of all colors, all happily screaming their heads off.

But the park, too, has been downhill and up. My downstairs neighbor in the Richelieu—although these days we just call it, fondly, "the House"—is Nadia Merzliakow, one of those Clinton Hill eminences who knows everyone and is known by everyone, to the point that bus drivers on the B52 line hold up traffic to yell hi to her when they see her out walking her dog. Nadia came to Clinton Hill from Manhattan in 1978, unenthusiastically, she's the first to admit, but once she was here she fell in love with the place and "grew deeply involved." The Clinton Hill she first encountered was very different. "It was tough. Lots of muggings. Lots of crime." And through her first decade in the neighborhood she watched Underwood Park go from bad to dreadful. "It was filthy. Totally neglected. The city had given up on it!" The park was no place to take children, or set foot in yourself. The Graham Home, its south wall now comprising the park's northern border, featured hookers displaying their wares in the generous windows. By 1993, two of Nadia's neighbors had had it, and with them she formed a brigade, perhaps five or six people in all. On their own time, at their own expense, without a shred of help from the city, they cleaned Underwood Park every Sunday for years, while their dogs played together. It's probably entirely due to them that in 1997 the city finally came back and renovated the park and provided the funds to maintain it.

"One summer my cousin from Bulgaria came to stay," recalls Nadia. "I would take her to the park with me to clean. She was absolutely *flabbergasted* that Americans would do that!—that they would go out and do that for their community. It was a *revelation* to her. When she went back to Bulgaria she was telling everybody, and it became a big story. She went to the United States to clean parks!"

Nadia and I talk about other things in Clinton Hill that have changed, and other things that really haven't. There's still plenty of drug dealing—you just don't see it so much unless you walk three blocks east to Grand Avenue. And there are still brothels, though the Graham Home is now pricey condos. The "Washington Hotel Apartments" on Washington at the corner of Greene is a brothel. Nadia knows because when she still smoked, she bought her cigarettes there from their lobby's machine, if it was late and the bodega was closed. "Everybody would say, How dare

you! And I'd say, I don't care, I just want my cigarettes!"
Another time, when Nadia was waiting for the bus at
Greene and Washington, very early in the morning, to go to
her pool for a swim, a man came running down the sidewalk stark naked and screaming that hookers had stolen
his clothes. "I had a towel to go swimming, so I threw it to
him and said, Hey! Cover yourself up. Then he said, I got
no money! So I gave him my bus fare. Then the bus came
and I don't know what happened. I left him my towel." Of
course, the bus driver knew Nadia, and let her get on without paying her fare.

We talk for so long that when I go back upstairs Dexter
is up from his nap and impatient to go to the park, with his
new plastic baseball and bat. My husband and I force him
into a jacket, but the day has turned warm—we can finally
suspect that the winter is ending. It's Sunday, and the park
is hopping. As much of our pleasure comes from reuniting
with friends we haven't seen in a season as from throwing
the baseball to Dexter and then chasing it (as it rolls east).
Underwood Park, from the very beginning, has reminded
me of a piazza, a little town square. It's the only public
space in the city that has given me friends that I cherish,
and the means to retain them, as well. Now that we're parents we're so busy, we can never do things, we can never
see people . . . except for our comrades of Underwood
Park. Here we constantly meet, in the interstices between
what we imagine makes up our "real" lives, but this life, we

have to admit—this endless throwing and retrieving of a ball, this endless cycle of shade trees to acorns to the winter hiatus from which our kids burst, metamorphosed completely, while we try to believe we ourselves haven't aged—is the real life: the repetitive rhythm, the onrush of time.

THE POOL AT THE ST. GEORGE HOTEL
Rachel Cline

EVERY SO OFTEN, someone stops me on Clark Street to ask directions to the subway. It always takes me a second or two to understand that although the entrance to the 2 and 3 train is *right there*, it is all but invisible. To get to the underground platform, you have to take one of three lumbering elevators at the back of what was once the lobby of the St. George Hotel. There are no green- or red-glass globes to signal "subway," and the building's battered marquees reveal nothing about the subterranean worlds contained therein.

It must be hard to imagine that the anonymous warren of delis, fast-food stands, and florists one must walk through to get to the turnstiles was, in its heyday, the public face of a fine hotel—not just fine, splendid. Established in 1884, the St. George could claim author Thomas Wolfe, abolitionist Henry Beecher, and presidents Kennedy, Truman, and Roosevelt (F. D.) among its guests. People actually came in from Manhattan to dance under the chameleonic lights of its "world-renowned" Colorama

Ballroom. After the addition of the tower building in 1929, the St. George was the largest hotel in New York City and also, just briefly, the tallest building in Brooklyn. The complex included a restaurant, a bar, a movie theater, fourteen ballrooms and banquet halls, and a health spa; there was even something billed as a "picturesque Italian village."

During the '60s and '70s—the era of my childhood—the St. George went downhill. Its tenants became an uncomfortable mix of the indigent and the elderly, and the then-owners ("a group of nationalist Chinese investors," wrote the *New York Times*) allowed fixtures and services to decay. The grand lobby furniture was dismantled and sold off, prompting the building's few remaining lifelong residents to reminisce about the days when one could call down to the desk for anything from a cheese sandwich to a diamond ring. In 1980, there was a disastrous attempt to convert its rooms to luxury condominiums (lawsuits ensued). Finally, in 1995, a sixteen-alarm fire devastated the place, paving the way for its current incarnation as a dormitory for local college students. I sometimes see them hanging around in front, smoking cigarettes in their pajamas.

THE visible landscape of Brooklyn Heights is much the same as it was in my childhood, which is a large part of why I moved back to the neighborhood after almost twenty years. I can walk down any street and look through the eyes of an earlier self: at age six, a manhole cover suggests a hidden world of trolls and tunnels; at eleven, the service entrance to my old building looks like a great place from which to spy; and at seventeen, I walk down Pierrepont Street singing rueful Bob Dylan lyrics to myself. But at the corner of Clark and Henry streets, I am most definitely nine years old, approaching the St. George newsstand with sixty-five cents in my hand. I will leave my whole allowance in the worn wooden dish above the pile of *Journal Americans*, and turn back toward Henry Street with a Van Houten bar, a packet of Adams Sour Apple Gum, and the latest issues of *Superman* and *Pep*. Before returning to the street, I will stop for a moment to smell the warm air rising up from the white-tiled stairway near the turnstiles—bay rum and iodine, sawdust and laundry. A sign above the banister reads "To Pool."

The St. George Pool, its salty greenish water fed by underground wells at the rate of 650 gallons per minute, was certainly the first wonder of my Brooklyn-based world.

At that time in my life, my best friend, Barbara, and I both lived a block away from the St. George. Barbara's Uncle Max, a neighborhood fixture then in his eighties and, I suspect, nobody's uncle, was a regular at the underground spa and occasionally brought us both along for the afternoon. He paid our admission fees to a clerk in the dark green, quasi-military serge of the hotel's bell staff and dropped us off at the service window where we were each given a scratchy, aggressively disinfected white towel. Barbara also received a hideous one-piece "bathing costume" in the smallest available size. Luckily, even the extra small was still too big for me and I got to wear the "poorboy" turtleneck suit my mother had brought home from B. Altman. (It was 1966; my turtleneck bathing suit was so *tuff*!)

Properly equipped, Barbara and I went alone to the ladies' locker room, stopping to gawk and marvel at the antique reducing machines at its entrance: one of them applied a vibrating hip sling; another concealed all but the head of its victim in a zip-front canvas tent. We also studied the black-and-white photographs on the walls, which memorialized pool visits by Esther Williams, Johnny Weismuller, Buster Crabbe, and other patron saints of American physical culture. This place had once been a true spa, a temple of health! But even by 1966 standards, its interpretation of that concept seemed off by a shade: Uncle Max was allowed to smoke cigars while taking the vapors, for one thing. For another, the water in the pool was pumped in from a natural source. Consider it. The Gowanus Canal?

The salinity of the water was also part of the spa concept. In addition to soothing aching muscles and restoring lost electrolytes, it was supposed to aid buoyancy. This I remember because floating was a sore point for me— Barbara said a bar of Ivory soap was purer than I was. Sadly, even at the St. George, I sank. The gilded ceiling looked just as glorious viewed from the depths, I told myself, sulkily.

The St. George Pool was only thirty-two years old when I first visited, but its origins seemed mythically distant— as far off as the vision of Babylon or Byzantium that had inspired its exuberant décor: old postcards show a mirrored, mosaic-wrapped room three stories high. In my memory, those mosaics are green-and-gold pictures of mermaids and athletes cavorting amid stylized waves, but my memory is not always reliable.

ALTHOUGH my first visits to the pool were with Barbara and Max, my most vivid memory is of an outing with my comrades from the Heights and Hills day camp. We were a group of twenty or thirty kids, most of us under the age of ten, who, on summer weekdays, would set off in our yellow school bus for outdoor recreations (Dyker Beach, Staten Island's Clove Lake, or the immense but banal public pool in Sunset Park). On the bus, we traded Beatles cards, played hand-clapping games, and sang gospel songs, although I doubt there were many Baptists in the party. The Heights (and hills) were funkier then than now—plenty of bohemians like my parents, and immigrants like my Greek babysitter, and divorcée moms like those of my three best friends from P.S. 8. There were also some—though not very many—people of color. In any case, one day we all went to the St. George. I guess the bus was being repaired, or maybe it was raining.

We were hustled through the changing process and

shooed past the fascinations of steam room and sun lamp, pinball machine and diving boards one, two, and three. The pool was unusually crowded that day and we were told to stay in the shallow end but, having had the run of the place on past visits, I was unwilling to be penned. I could not float, but I could swim like a fish underwater, and I set off for the deep end planning to cannonball off the forbidden high dive.

Approaching midpool, I came up for air, and, treading water, caught sight of some older boys, laughing and ignoring the "No Horseplay" signs near the four-foot mark. My eye was drawn to one boy in particular who wore an ivory necklace that stood out against his brown skin. I didn't know what a crucifix was (my bohemian parents were also atheists), but I wanted to admire the thing, which vaguely resembled the strands of dried seeds and pods my mother often wore. I *did* know what a boy was then, but not enough to be shy about approaching one. And so I dove back underwater and emerged slick and giggling at the side of my new idol, the better to gaze at him. I think I may have even reached up to touch it.

The Catholic boy at the four-foot mark, perhaps shy, or perhaps not a native speaker of English, responded by silently scooping me up into his arms and then dropping me back into the water from what felt like a heavenly height. Do it again, I said! Again! Again! And he did. Was he just too kind to refuse me? Was he inspired by our pagan surroundings or invigorated by the health-giving powers of those waters? It doesn't matter: he gave me ecstasy, and I never saw him again. (Unless I have—years later, I came across a reminiscence written by golden-skinned, Catholic-reared actor Jimmy Smits who, with his boyhood pals from East New York, also used to hang out at the St. George Pool. Not only arrestingly handsome, Mr. Smits would have been eleven years old that summer, so it delights me to imagine that it was he who sent me flying.)

Today, what remains of the St. George Pool is entombed within a generic private health club. Half of its basin has been filled in and made into a basketball court, the mosaics are muffled behind plaster and paint, and the water they want you to swim in makes your skin smell like Comet for days. And yet when neighborhood newcomers ask me for directions to the "red line" subway, I sometimes look at them in disbelief. Don't they remember? Those mosaics? That crucifix? Those arms? They do not. But I saw God, there, when I was nine, not so far from where the IRT still stops.

YOU CAN'T GO HOME AGAIN
John Burnham Schwartz

AROUND A DECADE ago, I called my father to tell him that
my wife and I were moving from Manhattan to Brooklyn.
His response was interesting: "Over my dead body," he
said. He was joking, I think, and assumed that I was too.
Discovering that I was in fact serious, he fell into a bewil-
dered silence.

"Dad," I explained. "Brooklyn's different now."

But he seemed neither to believe me nor to be comforted by my optimism. Perhaps this was because he was
speaking from his lovely home in Los Angeles, where the
sun was shining and depression is generally considered a
state of the mind, rather than of the wallet. Or perhaps his
reaction to my news had nothing at all to do with where he
found himself then, but rather with where he'd once been,
long ago. For my father, my moving to Brooklyn was
inevitably personal: he'd grown up in Brownsville, a tough,
insular, Jewish working-class community that stood lower
on the socioeconomic pecking order than even the Lower
East Side.

Brownsville: the name conjures its history, the opposite of brightness. Though the place was named not for the drab color but for a real estate speculator, Charles Brown, a would-be Trump of his day, who, in 1861, purchased a large parcel of land out on the jagged eastern edge of Brooklyn, and started building shacks in the hope of attracting Jews from Manhattan. The shacks became tenements, and the Jews—"middle-class" Jews, who were poor, and "poor" Jews, who were still poorer—came to live in them. Industry, or some simulacrum of it, soon followed, and by the turn of the century Brownsville was home to the largest concentration of Jews—mostly refugees and immigrants from Eastern Europe—in the United States. *Brunzvil,* the old people called it in the Yiddish they'd brought from their homelands, and for them and their children it remained forever a place out on the eastern reaches, far in mind, if not in literal miles, from "the city" that was New York and, it seemed then, America.

My father's house was on Ralph Avenue between Eastern Parkway and St. John's Place. My grandfather was an insurance broker and self-employed lawyer—which left them still poor, but a half-step up the economic ladder from the families of the housepainters, carpenters, plasterers, and bricklayers who used to gather daily on the corners along Pitkin Avenue to talk jobs and union gossip in the hotly politicized years of the thirties. Socialism was in the air. No one had any money—not the Jews, and not the Italians or the Irish who, hungry for work too, congregated on their own street corners just a few blocks away. Ethnicity was their difference, but also what they shared. There was violence, of course, but generally it was local to each group; the Jews of Brownsville could lay claim to Louis Lepke and Abe Reles, those infamous mobsters of Murder Inc., and, considerably lower down the food chain, to the Amboy Dukes gang. The less fierce of the Jewish kids in the neighborhood had "clubs"—for a while, my father was president of the Cherokees—whose ragtag members spent their days playing baseball and punchball for sums of money which, however paltry, always seemed worth fighting for.

My father's unhappiness as a kid in Brownsville, like all childhood unhappiness everywhere, had its particular roots. While he was president of the Cherokees, the boys used to hold their club meetings in the dank, unfinished basement of his house. He was their leader—until, one day, he decided that for the Cherokees to play ball against a rival club that had soundly beaten them before was a form of economic suicide; they were playing for money and were sure to lose. A born pessimist, he wanted no part of it. But his fellow club members were more optimistic and wanted to play. My father would not relent, which led to a fistfight, and, more or less immediately, to his becoming something of a social pariah, an exile in his own land. Which only shows, among other things, that there is more than one variety of poverty in the world—or, for that matter, in a neighborhood. By the time he was a teenager, my father had bitterly tasted a couple of them.

All this was a very long time ago, of course. But talking with my dad about those days, the past inevitably becomes present, a kind of haunting; even in sunny Los Angeles, he carries Brownsville with him.

In 1948, when he was fifteen, his family moved to a house in Jamaica, Queens. For Brownsville Jews of my grandparents' generation, this was the great leap forward. Prosperity had trickled down from the war, and given the opportunity, one family after another tore up roots and fled East Brooklyn. In their wake, they left already run-down tenements that would be filled by those poorer than themselves. These new immigrants—blacks from the American South and the Caribbean islands, Hispanics from Puerto Rico and Central America—would form the underprivileged and unseen army that would occupy the vast municipal housing projects of the urban social experiments of the next three decades, as Brownsville inexorably died.

But that death was not my father's story. My father's story, in 1948, was Queens, and the best thing about Queens was that it wasn't Brooklyn. It was a stepping stone, a way station: next stop, somewhere else. The only goal my father can remember from that time was to keep going. Which he did—eventually attending Yale Law School on a scholarship, marrying a beautiful blonde whose own childhood had glamorously been spent in foreign countries, and raising his kids in a large comfortable apart-

ment on the Upper East Side. Was there ever a place more
remote from Brownsville than the Upper East Side? From
my father's perspective, still after all those years, he'd gotten us *out*—a reverse exodus of heroic proportions, mixed
with dashes of startling good luck—and the idea that a son
of his would choose to live in the Old Country, where he'd
been poor and miserable, was something he couldn't quite
fathom or accept.

BEFORE we said good-bye on the phone that day, he asked
me if I'd ever read *A Walker in the City*, Alfred Kazin's
memoir of growing up in Brownsville during the Depression. I admitted that I hadn't. After all, thanks in part to my
father, I'd been raised a Manhattanite to my bones. At that
point, my wife and I knew hardly anything about Brooklyn
except that, in the endless pursuit of more space and, we
hoped, a better life, we intended to move there.

"Well, you should read it," my father urged me. "Kazin
was older, but when I was growing up there it was just the
way he described it. If that doesn't wise you up about
Brooklyn, nothing will. Go out and get a copy."

I took his advice, and wasn't sorry I did. I have the book
with me now. It was published in 1951, when its author—
already an extraordinary (and largely self-taught) literary
critic—was thirty-six. Here are its haunting first lines:

"Every time I go back to Brownsville it is as if I had
never been away. From the moment I step off the train at

Rockaway Avenue and smell the leak out of the men's room, then the pickles from the stand just below the subway steps, an instant rage comes over me, mixed with dread and some unexpected tenderness."

Rage and dread and unexpected tenderness: yes, I thought with a sudden jolt of recognition, he's describing my father's voice on the phone that day, talking about Brooklyn. Brooklyn understandably being for my dad Brownsville, circa 1942, say, the Brooklyn he knew and couldn't forget. (On that indelible map drawn on the inside of his eyelids one would have to include Ebbets Field, home to the Brooklyn Dodgers; but Ebbets Field, of course, is long gone, and the Dodgers, like my father, fled to Los Angeles.)

Kazin again:

"Every sound from the street roared and trembled at our windows—a mother feeding her child on the doorstep, the screech of the trolley cars on Rockaway Avenue, the eternal smash of a handball against the wall of our house, the clatter of *der italyéner's* cart packed with watermelons, the singsong of the old clothes men walking Chester Street . . ."

By the time of the writer's revisitation in the late forties, around the time my father was leaving Brownsville for good, many of the old shops that both men had known—the fruit and vegetable stands and the dry goods stores and the luggage shops—had been replaced by second-hand furniture stores, as if the old way of life were being disposed of in one great stoop sale.

What he was writing even then, it's clear, was a eulogy,

wonderfully and terribly bittersweet. Ambivalence about
the history of that place and a longing for what it once had
been pervade every line of the book. For men like Kazin
and my father, such ambivalence was their birthright, well-
earned. And what are birthrights for, if not to be passed on
to one's children?

KAZIN is dead now, and my father is seventy-four. So much
distance traveled; and Brownsville itself, of course, an
utterly changed neighborhood racially and economically,
having been killed, and then, painfully, slowly, resuscitated
from its own blood and ashes.

Unlike Kazin, the walker and wanderer, my father has
been back exactly twice. The first time, in 1981, following
his divorce and his move to Los Angeles, he was accompanied to Brooklyn by his then-girlfriend, a California native,
who, I imagine, must have been mystified and alarmed as
my father—his heart beginning to hammer with the dread
and rage and tenderness that Kazin had experienced thirty
years before him—turned the rental car left from Eastern
Parkway onto Ralph Avenue. Here was the old block: the
tenement row houses made of brick, the scarred stoops and
rusted fire escapes. Except that they were gone. In their
place, my father later told me, stood three crumbling,
cheaply painted buildings surrounded by a city of rubble.
Entire blocks of housing projects razed, burned out, gutted.
Streets on which he used to play stickball and punchball

buried under mountains of trash. The neighborhood was African-American and Caribbean-American, poor beyond reckoning; and then, as he drove away from it, abruptly the streets were populated by nothing but Orthodox Jews. As if everything but that invisible racial dividing line—the barrier of fear and prejudice that people, wherever they are, somehow never forget how to erect against those who are different—had failed to survive my father's memory of the place.

And then, sixteen years later, soon after my wife and I had set up house on Hicks Street in Brooklyn, my father was in town on business, and he asked me if I would be interested in driving out with him to his old neighborhood, to see what was there. I looked at him, surprised, and said certainly, I'd be interested. I was a Brooklyn resident, after all, and Brownsville seemed not so far away as it once had.

A sunny, hot day. We drove with the windows open, car horns and exhaust flooding over us, and on the seat beside me my father looked not so much grim as anxious. We took the long route, not knowing any better: from Grand Army Plaza, we made our way far, far down Eastern Parkway; and then, finally, on Ralph Avenue, we turned left. On the block where, he told me, he'd once lived, we stopped the car and looked around. For a long time neither of us said a word. Then slowly my father shook his head.

A row of painted brick houses. The rubble around them cleared. The street not clean, but passable. Children were playing.

The block, which sixteen years earlier had appeared dead to him, was alive again.

"It's coming back," my father said, more to himself than to me. He seemed at once incredulous and humbled.

"I told you, Dad. Brooklyn's different now."

He looked at me as if he had no idea know what I was talking about. Then he nodded. He put his hand on my shoulder and said, "Let's go back to your place. Let's go home."

HOME AT LAST

Dinaw Mengestu

AT TWENTY-ONE I moved to Brooklyn hoping that it would be the last move I would ever make—that it would, with the gradual accumulation of time, memory, and possessions, become that place I instinctively reverted back to when asked, "So, where are you from?" I was born in Ethiopia like my parents and their parents before them, but it would be a lie to say I was *from* Ethiopia, having left the country when I was only two years old following a military coup and civil war, losing in the process the language and any direct memory of the family and culture I had been born into. I simply am Ethiopian, without the necessary "from" that serves as the final assurance of our identity and origin.

Since leaving Addis Ababa in 1980, I've lived in Peoria, Illinois; in a suburb of Chicago; and then finally, before moving to Brooklyn, in Washington, D.C., the de facto capital of the Ethiopian immigrant. Others, I know, have moved much more often and across much greater distances. I've only known a few people, however, that have grown up with the oddly permanent feeling of having lost and abandoned a home that you never, in fact, really knew, a feeling that has nothing to do with apartments, houses, or miles, but rather the sense that no matter how far you travel, or how long you stay still, there is no place that you can always return to, no place where you fully belong. My parents, for all that they had given up by leaving Ethiopia, at least had the certainty that they had come from some place. They knew the country's language and culture, had met outside of coffee shops along Addis's main boulevard in the early days of their relationship, and as a result, regardless of how mangled by violence Ethiopia later became, it was irrevocably and ultimately theirs. Growing up, one of my father's favorite sayings was, "Remember, you are Ethiopian," even though, of course, there was nothing for me to remember apart from the bits of nostalgia and culture my parents had imparted. What remained had less to do with the idea that I was from Ethiopia and more to do with the fact that I was not from America.

I can't say when exactly I first became aware of that feeling—that I was always going to and never from—but surely I must have felt it during those first years in Peoria, with my parents, sister, and me always sitting on the edge of whatever context we were now supposed to be a part of, whether it was the all-white Southern Baptist Church we went to every weekend, or the nearly all-white Catholic schools my sister and I attended first in Peoria and then again in Chicago at my parents' insistence. By that point my father, haunted by the death of his brother during the revolution and the ensuing loss of the country he had always assumed he would live and die in, had taken to long evening walks that he eventually let me accompany him on. Back then he had a habit of sometimes whispering his brother's name as he walked ("Shibrew," he would mutter) or whistling the tunes of Amharic songs that I had never known. He always walked with both hands firmly clasped behind his back, as if his grief, transformed into something real and physical, could be grasped and secured in the palms of his hands. That was where I first learned what it meant to lose and be alone. The lesson would be reinforced over the years whenever I caught sight of my mother sitting by herself on a Sunday afternoon, staring silently out of our living room's picture window, recalling, perhaps, her father who had died after she left, or her mother, four sisters, and one brother in Ethiopia—or else recalling nothing at all because there was no one to visit her, no one to call or see. We had been stripped bare here in America, our lives confined to small towns and urban suburbs. We had sacrificed precisely those things that can never be compensated for or repaid—parents, siblings, culture, a memory to a place that dates back more than half a generation. It's easy to see now how even as a family we were isolated from one another—my parents tied and lost to their past; my sister and I irrevocably assimilated. For years we were strangers even among ourselves.

*   *   *

BY the time I arrived in Brooklyn I had little interest in where I actually landed. I had just graduated college and had had enough of the fights and arguments about not being "black" enough, as well as the earlier fights in high school hallways and street corners that were fought for simply being black. Now it was enough, I wanted to believe, to simply be, to say I was in Brooklyn and Brooklyn was home. It wasn't until after I had signed the lease on my apartment that I even learned the name of the neighborhood I had moved into: Kensington, a distinctly regal name at a price that I could afford; it was perfect, in other words, for an eager and poor writer with inflated ambitions and no sense of where he belonged.

After less than a month of living in Kensington I had covered almost all of the neighborhood's streets, deliberately committing their layouts and routines to memory in a first attempt at assimilation. There was an obvious and deliberate echo to my walks, a self-conscious reenactment of my father's routine that I adopted to stave off some of my own emptiness. It wasn't just that I didn't have any deep personal relationships here, it was that I had chosen this city as the place to redefine, to ground, to secure my place in the world. If I could bind myself to Kensington physically, if I could memorize and mentally reproduce in accurate detail the various shades of the houses on a particular block, then I could stake my own claim to it, and in doing so, no one could tell me who I was or that I didn't belong.

On my early-morning walks to the F train I passed in
succession a Latin American restaurant and grocery store,
a Chinese fish market, a Halal butcher shop, followed by a
series of Pakistani and Bangladeshi takeout restaurants.
This cluster of restaurants on the corner of Church and
McDonald, I later learned, sold five-dollar plates of lamb
and chicken biryani in portions large enough to hold me
over for a day, and in more financially desperate times, two
days. Similarly, I learned that the butcher and fish shop
delivery trucks arrived on most days just as I was making
my way to the train. If I had time, I found it hard not to
stand and stare at the refrigerated trucks with their calf
and sheep carcasses dangling from hooks, or at the tanks of
newly arrived bass and catfish flapping around in a shallow
pool of water just deep enough to keep them alive.

It didn't take long for me to develop a fierce loyalty to
Kensington, to think of the neighborhood and my place
in it as emblematic of a grander immigrant narrative. In
response to that loyalty, I promised to host a "Kensington
night" for the handful of new friends that I eventually
made in the city, an evening that would have been com-
prised of five-dollar lamb biryani followed by two-dollar
Budweisers at Denny's, the neighborhood's only full-
fledged bar—a defunct Irish pub complete with terribly
dim lighting and wooden booths. I never hosted a Kensington night, however, no doubt in part because I had established my own private relationship to the neighborhood,
one that could never be shared with others in a single

evening of cheap South Asian food and beer. I knew the hours of the call of the muezzin that rang from the mosque a block away from my apartment. I heard it in my bedroom every morning, afternoon, and evening, and if I was writing when it called out, I learned that it was better to simply stop and admire it. My landlord's father, an old gray-haired Chinese immigrant who spoke no English, gradually smiled at me as I came and went, just as I learned to say hello, as politely as possible, in Mandarin every time I saw him. The men behind the counters of the Bangladeshi takeout places now knew me by sight. A few, on occasion, slipped an extra dollop of vegetables or rice into my to-go container, perhaps because they worried that I wasn't eating enough. One in particular, who was roughly my age, spoke little English, and smiled wholeheartedly whenever I came in, gave me presweetened tea and free bread, a gesture that I took to be an acknowledgment that, at least for him, I had earned my own, albeit marginal, place here.

And so instead of sitting with friends in a brightly lit fluorescent restaurant with cafeteria-style service, I found myself night after night quietly walking around the neighborhood in between sporadic fits of writing. Kensington was no more beautiful by night than by day, and perhaps this very absence of grandeur allowed me to feel more at ease wandering its streets at night. The haphazard gathering of immigrants in Kensington had turned it into a place that even someone like me, haunted and conscious of race and identity at every turn, could slip and blend into.

Inevitably on my way home I returned to the corner of Church and McDonald with its glut of identical restaurants. On warm nights, I had found it was the perfect spot to stand and admire not only what Kensington had become with the most recent wave of migration, but what any close-knit community—whether its people came here one hundred years ago from Europe or a decade ago from Africa, Asia, or the Caribbean—has provided throughout Brooklyn's history: a second home. There, on that corner, made up of five competing South Asian restaurants of roughly equal quality, dozens of Pakistani and Bangladeshi men gathered one night after another to drink chai out of paper cups. The men stood there talking for hours, huddled in factions built in part, I imagine, around restaurant loyalties. Some nights I sat in one of the restaurants and watched from a corner table with a book in hand as an artificial prop. A few of the men always stared, curious no doubt as to what I was doing there. Even though I lived in Kensington, when it came to evening gatherings like this, I was the foreigner and tourist. On other nights I ordered my own cup of tea and stood a few feet away on the edge of the sidewalk, near the subway entrance or at the bus stop, and silently stared. I had seen communal scenes like this before, especially while living in Washington, D.C., where there always seemed to be a cluster of Ethiopians, my age or older, gathered together outside coffee shops and bars all over the city, talking in Amharic with an ease and fluency that I admired and envied. They told jokes that didn't require explanation and debated arguments that were decades in the making. All of this was coupled with the familiarity and comfort of speaking in our native tongue. At any given moment, they could have told you without hesitancy where they were from. And so I had watched, hardly understanding a word, hoping somehow that the simple act of association and observation was enough to draw me into the fold.

Here, then, was a similar scene, this one played out on a Brooklyn corner with a culture and history different from the one I had been born into, but familiar to me nonetheless. The men on that corner in Kensington, just like the people I had known throughout my life, were immigrants in the most complete sense of the word—their loyalties still firmly attached to the countries they had left one, five, or twenty years earlier. If there was one thing I admired most about them, it was that they had succeeded, at least partly, in re-creating in Brooklyn some of what they had lost when they left their countries of origin. Unlike the solitary and private walks my father and I took, each of us buried deep in thoughts that had nowhere to go, this nightly gathering of Pakistani and Bangladeshi men was a makeshift reenactment of home. Farther down the road from where they stood were the few remaining remnants of the neighborhood's older Jewish community—one synagogue, a kosher deli—proof, if one was ever needed, that Brooklyn is always reinventing itself, that there is room here for us all.

While the men stood outside on the corner, their numbers gradually increasing until they spilled out into the street as they talked loudly among themselves, I once again played my own familiar role of quiet, jealous observer and secret admirer. I have no idea what those men talked about, if they discussed politics, sex, or petty complaints about work. It never mattered anyway. The substance of the conversations belonged to them, and I couldn't have cared less. What I had wanted and found in them, what I admired and adored about Kensington, was the assertion that we can rebuild and remake ourselves and our communities over and over again, in no small part because there have always been corners in Brooklyn to do so on. I stood on that corner night after night for the most obvious of reasons—to be reminded of a way of life that persists regardless of context; to feel, however foolishly, that I too was attached to something.

ACKNOWLEDGMENTS

THE EDITORS would like to thank the contributors for their beautifully told stories, for their wit and creativity, and, above all, for their generosity, without which this book would not exist. Thanks also to Daniel Goldstein and Develop, Don't Destroy Brooklyn; Geoff Kloske, Megan Lynch, Sarah Bowlin, Rick Pascocello, Leslie Schwartz, Ashley Fisher, Charles Bjorklund, Benjamin Gibson, and the terrific team at Riverhead; Tina Bennett and Svetlana Katz at Janklow & Nesbit; Anna Wintour, Laurie Jones, Shelley Wanger, Dodie Kazanjian, Abigail Walch, Eve Mac-Sweeney, Megan O'Grady, Adam Green, Megan Conway, Kimberly Straub, Mark Rozzo, David Remnick, Cressida Leyshon, Sean Howe, Jonathan Bennet, Deb Garrison, and Daniel Menaker. Individually, Chris Knutsen is grateful to his father and mother, for not taking the Brooklyn out of themselves, and to the much adored Nuar, Isadora, and—especially—Sabine, who was not born in time to be thanked in the last anthology. Valerie Steiker would like to thank Stephanie Steiker, Dan Lane, Erika Kawalek, Tyler Maroney, Daphne Beal, Sean Wilsey, Christiane Mack, Marko MacPherson, and most of all her beloved husband and son, Matthew Lane and Julian Steiker Lane, for making Brooklyn feel like home.

ABOUT THE CONTRIBUTORS

EMILY BARTON is the author of the bestselling historical novel *Brookland* as well as *The Testament of Yves Gundron*, which won the Bard Fiction Prize and a Michener-Copernicus Fellowship, was named a *New York Times* Notable Book, and was nominated for the Guardian Fiction Prize. Her fiction has appeared in *Story*, *American Short Fiction*, and *Conjunctions*. In 2006, she received a Guggenheim Fellowship and a grant from the National Endowment for the Arts.

SUSAN CHOI is the author of the novels *American Woman*, which was a finalist for the Pulitzer Prize, and *The Foreign Student*, which won the Asian-American Literary Award for Fiction. With David Remnick, she edited an anthology of fiction entitled *Wonderful Town: New York Stories from the* New Yorker. Her new novel is *A Person of Interest*, from Viking. She lives in Brooklyn with her husband and sons.

RACHEL CLINE is the author of the novel *What to Keep*. Her second novel, *My Liar*, is forthcoming from Random House. She lives in Brooklyn Heights.

PHILIP DRAY is the author of *At the Hands of Persons Unknown: The Lynching of Black America*, which received the Robert F. Kennedy Memorial Book Award and the Southern Book Critics Circle Award for Nonfiction, and was a finalist for the Los Angeles Times Book Award and the Pulitzer Prize. He also wrote *Stealing God's Thunder: Benjamin Franklin's Lightning Rod and the Invention of America*, and was coauthor of *We Are Not Afraid: The Story of Goodman, Schwerner, and Chaney, and the Civil Rights Campaign for Mississippi*, which was a *New York Times* Notable Book. He lives in Brooklyn.

JENNIFER EGAN is the author of three novels, *The Invisible Circus*, *Look at Me* (a finalist for the National Book Award), and the bestselling *The Keep*, as well as a short story collection, *Emerald City*. She has published short fiction in the *New Yorker*, *Harper's*, *McSweeney's*, and *Ploughshares*, among others, and her journalism appears frequently in the *New York Times Magazine*. She lives in Fort Greene, Brooklyn.

ELIZABETH GAFFNEY is the author of *Metropolis* and the editor at large of *A Public Space*.

COLIN HARRISON is a senior editor at Scribner and was formerly the deputy editor of *Harper's*. He is the author of six novels: *The Finder*, to be published in spring 2008, *The Havana Room*, *Afterburn*, *Manhattan Nocturne*, *Bodies Electric*, and *Break and Enter*. He lives in Brooklyn with his wife, the writer Kathryn Harrison, and their three children.

JOANNA HERSHON is the author of three novels: *Swimming*, *The Outside of August*, and *The German Bride*, which is forthcoming in spring 2008. Her short fiction has been published in *One Story* and the *Virginia Quarterly Review*. She lives in Brooklyn with her husband, the painter Derek Buckner, and their twin sons.

JONATHAN LETHEM is the author of six novels, including the bestsellers *You Don't Love Me Yet*, *The Fortress of Solitude*, and *Motherless Brooklyn*, which won the National Book Critics Circle Award. He lives in Brooklyn and Maine.

PHILLIP LOPATE is the author of three essay collections: *Bachelorhood*, *Against Joie de Vivre*, and *Portrait of My Body*; two novels, *Confessions of Summer* and *The Rug Merchant*; two poetry collections, *The Eyes Don't Always Want to Stay Open* and *The Daily Round*; and a memoir, *Being with Children*. His essays, fiction, and poetry have appeared in *The Best American Short Stories*, *The Best American Essays*, several Pushcart Prize annuals, and numerous other periodicals.

He has been awarded a John Simon Guggenheim Fellowship, a New York Public Library Center for Scholars and
Writers Fellowship, two National Endowment for the Arts
grants, and two New York Foundation for the Arts grants.
He currently holds the Adams Chair at Hofstra University,
where he is a professor of English, and also teaches in the
Bennington College MFA program. He lives in Brooklyn.

DINAW MENGESTU was born in Addis Ababa, Ethiopia, in
1978, and is the author of *The Beautiful Things That Heaven
Bears*. The recipient of a 2006 fellowship in fiction from
the New York Foundation for the Arts, he lives in Brooklyn.

LAWRENCE OSBORNE is the author of *The Accidental Con-
noisseur* and *The Naked Tourist*, both published by Farrar,
Straus and Giroux. His next book is about Bangkok. He
lives in Brooklyn.

KATIE ROIPHE is the author of the nonfiction works
Uncommon Arrangements, *The Morning After*, and *Last
Night in Paradise*, as well as the novel *Still She Haunts Me*.
She teaches in the Cultural Criticism and Reporting Pro-
gram at New York University and has written for numerous
publications, including *Harper's*, *Esquire*, the *New York
Times*, and *Vogue*. She lives in Brooklyn.

JOHN BURNHAM SCHWARTZ is the author of the novels *The
Commoner*, *Claire Marvel*, *Bicycle Days*, and *Reservation*

Road (now a major motion picture based on his screenplay from Focus Features). His work has been translated into fifteen languages and has appeared in numerous publications, including the *New York Times*, the *New Yorker*, the *Boston Globe*, and *Vogue*. He lives with his wife and son in Brooklyn.

VIJAY SESHADRI is the author of two books of poems, *Wild Kingdom* and *The Long Meadow*, both from Graywolf Press. His work has been widely published and recognized with a number of honors. He lives on Sackett Street in Brooklyn, and teaches at Sarah Lawrence College.

DARCEY STEINKE is the author of four novels, two of which were *New York Times* Notable Books. Her most recent book is a memoir, *Easter Everywhere*. Her Web project BlindSpot was included in the 2000 Whitney Biennial. She has contributed to *Spin*, *Vogue*, and the *New York Times Magazine*, among other places. She teaches in the graduate program of Columbia and the New School and lives in Brooklyn.

DARIN STRAUSS is the author of the international bestseller *Chang and Eng*, and the *New York Times* Notable Book *The Real McCoy*. He teaches writing at New York University, and was awarded a 2006 Guggenheim Fellowship in fiction writing. He lives in Brooklyn.

ALEXANDRA STYRON is the author of the novel *All the Finest Girls*. Her work has appeared in *Interview*, *Real*

Simple, and *Avenue*, as well as several anthologies. She lives in Park Slope, Brooklyn, with her husband and two children, and is at work on her second novel.

ROBERT SULLIVAN is the author of *Rats* and, most recently, *Cross Country: Fifteen Years and 90,000 Miles on the Roads and Interstates of America with Lewis and Clark, a Lot of Bad Motels, a Moving Van, Emily Post, Jack Kerouac, My Wife, My Mother-in-Law, Two Kids, and Enough Coffee to Kill an Elephant*. His books *The Meadowlands* and *A Whale Hunt* were both *New York Times* Notable Books. He is the recipient of a National Endowment for the Arts creative writing fellowship. A contributing editor to *Vogue*, he has written for *Condé Nast Traveler*, the *New Yorker*, *Dwell*, and the *New York Times Magazine*. He lives in Brooklyn.

LARA VAPNYAR emigrated from Russia to Brooklyn in 1994 and began publishing short stories in English in 2002. She is the author of the novel *Memoirs of a Muse* and the short story collection *There Are Jews in My House*, which was nominated for a Los Angeles Times Book Prize and the New York Public Library Young Lions Fiction Award, and received the National Foundation for Jewish Culture's prize for Jewish Fiction by Emerging Writers. Her work has appeared in the *New York Times*, *Vogue*, and the *New Yorker*. She lives on Staten Island with her husband and two children.

ABOUT THE EDITORS

CHRIS KNUTSEN is the coeditor *of Committed: Men Tell Stories of Love, Commitment, and Marriage*. A senior editor at *Vogue,* he previously worked at the *New Yorker* and Riverhead Books. He lives in Fort Greene, Brooklyn, with his wife and daughters.

VALERIE STEIKER is the author of *The Leopard Hat: A Daughter's Story*, a memoir of her Belgian-Jewish mother. The culture editor at *Vogue*, she previously worked at *Artforum* and the *New Yorker*. She lives in Brooklyn Heights with her husband and son.

CREDITS

Introduction by Phillip Lopate. Copyright © 2008 Phillip Lopate.

"I Hate Brighton Beach" by Lara Vapnyar. Copyright © 2008 Lara Vapnyar.

"Reading Lucy" by Jennifer Egan. Copyright © 2008 Jennifer Egan.

"Riding in Red Hook" by Lawrence Osborne. Copyright © 2008 Lawrence Osborne.

"A Sentimental Education" by Alexandra Styron. Copyright © 2008 Alexandra Styron.

"Brooklyn Wildlife" by Vijay Seshadri. Copyright © 2008 Vijay Seshadri.

"A Coney Island of the Mind" by Katie Roiphe. Copyright © 2008 Katie Roiphe.

"Ruckus Flatbush" by Jonathan Lethem. Copyright © 2008 Jonathan Lethem.

"Eli Miller's Seltzer Delivery Service" by Emily Barton. Copyright © 2008 Emily Barton.

"Brooklyn Pastoral" by Darcey Steinke. Copyright © 2008 Darcey Steinke.

"Diamonds" by Colin Harrison. Copyright © 2008 Colin Harrison.

"Make a Light" by Philip Dray. Copyright © 2008 Philip Dray.

"Bridges" by Joanna Hershon. Copyright © 2008 Joanna Hershon.

"A Windstorm in Downtown Brooklyn" by Robert Sullivan. Copyright © 2008 Robert Sullivan.